The BOYS' Book

HOW TO BE THE Best AT Everything

Written by Dominique Enright and Guy Macdonald
Illustrated by Niki Catlow
Edited by Samantha Barnes and Philippa Wingate

Grateful thanks to Ellen Bailey; Claire Buchan; Jamie Buchan;
Toby Buchan; Agnieszka Chojnowska; David Bann; Ray King;
Dr John L. Breen of the School of Oriental and African Studies,
University of London; and to the press offices of the London
embassies of Greece, Sweden, and the Russian Federation.

The BOYS' Book

HOW TO BE THE Best AT Everything

Buster Books

The Boys' Book: How To Be The Best At Everything is a revised and expanded edition of *How To Be The Best At Everything*, first published in 2004 by Buster Books, an imprint of Michael O'Mara Books Limited. It also includes material from *Children's Miscellany: Volume One, Children's Miscellany: Volume Two, Children's Miscellany: Volume Three* published in 2004, 2005, 2006 by Buster Books.

First published in Great Britain in 2006 by Buster Books, an imprint of Michael O'Mara Books Limited, 16 Lion Yard, Tremadoc Road, London SW4 7NQ

Text copyright © Buster Books 2004, 2005, 2006
Illustrations copyright © Buster Books 2004, 2005, 2006
Cover designed: www.blacksheep-uk.com
Cover illustration: Getty Images

A CIP catalogue record for this book is available from the British Library.

ISBN 10 digit: 1-905158-64-5
ISBN 13 digit: 978-1-905158-64-5

10 9 8 7 6 5 4 3 2 1

www.mombooks.com/busterbooks

Printed and bound in England by Clays Ltd, St Ives plc

The paper this book is printed on is certified by the Forest Stewardship Council. The printer holds FSC chain of custody SGS–COC–2061.

CONTENTS

HOW TO DO AN OLLIE

This technique is the basis for most other skateboarding tricks. It allows a skater to jump over an obstacle, or on to a step or low wall, while the whole time the board appears to stick to the skater's feet.

1. As you skate, place your back foot on the tail (back) of the board, and your front foot halfway between the nose (front) of the board and the tail.

2. Crouch in readiness to jump. Push down on the tail of the board with your back foot.

3. Now straighten your legs, effectively jumping into the air. The downward force on the tail will make the board come up with your front foot.

4. As the board rises, slide your front foot towards the nose. Then, with that foot, push down on the nose.

5. Lift your other foot to allow the tail to rise as the downward force is applied to the nose.

6. The board will now be level as you reach the peak of the jump. Then gravity takes hold, and you and the board come down.

7. As you descend, bend your legs again, to take up the impact of landing.

HOW TO INSULT SOMEONE AND GET AWAY WITH IT

With this list of posh put-downs you'll never be short of something to say to unsuspecting friends. And you'll never get into trouble because they won't be familiar with the words you are using. Even your teacher will be flabbergasted and impressed.

asinine (ass-in-ine) very stupid: 'What an asinine thing to do.'

blatherskite (blather-skite) a person who talks a load of nonsense: 'What a blatherskite you are.'

cacophony (ka-koff-funny) unpleasantly loud noise: 'What a cacophony my sister is making with her singing.'

discombobulate (dis-kom-bob-u-late) confuse: 'He was totally discombobulated by what I said.'

lollapalooza (lolla-palooza) a particularly attractive or impressive thing or person: 'He's no lollapalooza in his school uniform.'

noisome (noyzsome) stinking, extremely unpleasant: 'My brother's bedroom is very noisome.'

tawdry (tordry) something flashy but of rubbish quality: 'Auntie, what fabulously tawdry jewellery you are wearing.'

technophobe (tekno-fobe) someone who dislikes or fears new technology: 'My dad can't even answer his mobile phone. He's a real technophobe.'

temerity (tem-erity) extreme boldness and cheek: 'What temerity to insult people like this.'

HOW TO FLY A HELICOPTER

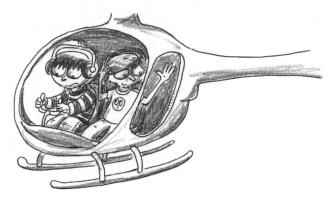

A helicopter can move up and down, forwards and backwards, and sideways. It can also rotate 360 degrees, stop in mid-air, and hover … and while hovering it can spin round. As a helicopter pilot you must be at your most alert to be able to operate and control the movement of the craft.

1. In one hand you have the collective pitch stick. This adjusts the main rotors so that the helicopter can go up and down. It also controls the engine speed.

2. In the other hand you have the cyclic pitch. This control makes the main rotor tilt so that it can pull the helicopter backwards, forwards or sideways.

3. Your feet rest on pedals that control the tail rotor. This allows the helicopter to turn to face any direction.

To perfect your flight and avoid embarrassing wild spins, dips this way and that, and jerky rises and drops in the air, you have to make sure that your hands and feet work together to make the helicopter do what you want it to do.

HOW TO PERFORM MAGIC

Here's a magic trick that is
guaranteed to fool everyone:

1. Before you perform the trick,
you need to make a trick card.
Cut a black king in half and glue it
to the front of the 10 of diamonds.
Position it half way across the 10
and slightly tilted to the right, as
shown here.

2. Next, take three cards from the
pack – your trick card, the 5 of hearts and the jack
of clubs.

3. Fan out the cards as shown below. Make sure the
jack is completely hidden behind the 5 of hearts, so

only the 10 of diamonds,
the king of spades and the
5 of hearts are showing.

4. Show the fan of cards to
your audience. Then close
the fan. Turn your hand
over and fan out the cards
again, holding them face
down.

5. Ask someone to pick out the king. They will probably
pick the middle card thinking it is the king. It won't be
the king; it will be the jack.

HOW TO SURVIVE IN SPACE

If you're very rich you could go to space for a holiday. The other way to get to space is to become an astronaut, and an astronaut must be the best at everything.

You have to wear a spacesuit while travelling on the space shuttle, but on the space station you can wear ordinary clothing. You'll spend time on board the space station growing plants, making crystals and performing experiments in near-zero gravity.

You will need to exercise frequently to minimize the loss of bone and muscle mass caused by weightlessness. Gym equipment is provided. During your free time, you can send e-mails home, play cards with fellow astronauts and admire the view of earth.

You will eat in the galley. The food is in containers attached to a tray which is in turn attached either to you or to a wall (otherwise your meal floats off). The meals themselves are not made up of tablets, though – you get proper appetizing food just like at home.

You will sleep in bunk-style sleeping quarters or, if there's not much room, in sleeping bags. These of course have to be attached to a wall or they will float about and you'll wake up in another part of the station.

As there's no washing machine aboard, you will need to take with you a great deal of clothing. Dirty clothes are sealed in plastic bags, in much the same way as all the rubbish is.

The toilet is fairly similar to those on earth. A steady flow of air moves through the unit when it is in use, carrying waste to a special container or into plastic bags. The plastic bags are then sealed. (Some of the waste might be returned to earth for laboratory analysis.)

To wash, you will have a freshwater hose to shower you and a vacuum hose to suck up all the water. In other words you use vacuum cleaners on yourself. You can't have a bath as the water will float about. This is very dangerous as it might short-circuit electrical equipment.

As for brushing your teeth – that can be a challenge, too. You have to make sure the toothpaste is well down on the bristles and you have to stop the water from running away.

You may have to perform spacewalks to complete your mission. This will involve getting into a spacesuit, which has been made to withstand flying debris and to protect astronauts from dramatic temperature changes (from −85°C in the shade to over 120°C in the hot sunlight).

The spacesuit has a pressurized atmosphere, a source of oxygen, a means of removing carbon dioxide, a temperature regulator, some protection against radiation, and the means to communicate at all times with ground control or the space station.

After going through depressurization procedures in the airlock, you'll step out. You are either attached by an air hose to the space station or you have a gas-propelled chair or unit that you can control so that you can go where you want, rather than drifting around helplessly.

HOW TO READ TEA LEAVES

Drink a cup of leaf tea from a plain white cup and leave a small amount of liquid in the bottom. Hold the cup in your left hand and swirl the liquid around three times in a clockwise direction. Make sure that the tea leaves reach the rim but don't spill over. Turn the cup upside down onto a saucer, letting the liquid drain away. After seven seconds, turn the cup back the right way up and hold it so that the handle points towards you.

Use the patterns created to predict the future, for example, if you see a wheel shape, that could mean your subject is going on a journey.

HOW TO LOSE YOUR HEAD

You will need a chair and table to sit at, with your
homework set out on the table. You must be wearing
a large shirt with buttons down
the front and a collar.

1. Sit down on the
chair. Unbutton your
shirt and pull the
neck of it up around
your head. Rebutton
the top three buttons
behind your neck,
with your head poking
forward. Make sure that your shirt is firmly tucked into your
trousers at the back. Shape the collar of your shirt (which is
now behind your head) into a neck-shaped circle.

2. Still sitting on your chair, duck your head under the
table. With your free hand make sure that the front of your
shirt collar is at least level with the tabletop, preferably
above it. Make sure, too, that the collar is still in a roughly
neck-shaped circle.

3. Now put your elbows up onto the edge of the table.
Pick up your pen in one hand, look busy and wait for
people to come in and see how your homework has made
you lose your head.

Think of other times when you can make a headless
appearance. It can be really funny at mealtimes, or at
a friend's party.

HOW TO MAKE A MAGIC CIRCLE

The magic circle, or Möbius strip, named after a German mathematician, is a loop with only one surface and one edge. Impossible? Well, here is how you make one:

1. Cut a strip of paper (try to keep the width even so that you have a long, thin rectangle like the one shown here). To make sure you tape the loop the right way, write A on the top right-hand corner, B on the top left, C on the bottom right, and D on the bottom left as shown here.

2. Hold the two ends in your hands, give the strip a half-twist by turning the end marked D and C upside down, then tape together the ends, A to D, B to C. Now you have your loop, like the one below.

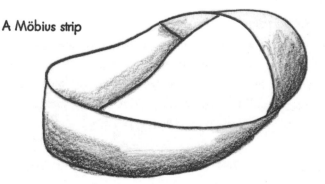

A Möbius strip

3. Now take a pen and, starting at any point, draw a line along the centre of the strip, continuing all the way until you reach the starting point of your line. You'll have drawn a line on both sides of the loop – but without lifting your pen or crossing any edge, which means the paper has only one side.

4. Take a highlighter and colour the edge of the strip. When you reach your starting point, you'll find that both edges are coloured, which means the strip only has one edge.

5. Now, with scissors, cut the Möbius strip along the central pen line that you drew earlier. It does not, as you'd expect, fall apart into two separate loops – instead you now have a single, larger, one-sided loop!

6. Draw a central line around the resulting loop and cut along it – can you predict what will happen?

HOW TO FIGHT OFF A CROCODILE

Crocodiles are efficient killing machines. They might seem slow, but they can move very quickly in the water and leap out very suddenly and at great speed.

1. If you're standing near a lake and a crocodile springs from the water towards you – run. And keep running for at least 15m (50ft). If you cannot run, try to get up on to the creature's back and stand on its neck to stop it from opening its jaws – crocodiles have weak jaw-opening muscles and you can hold their jaws shut without too much difficulty. On the other hand, their jaw-closing muscles are incredibly powerful and it is almost impossible to prise them open.

2. Alternatively, if you are in the water and a crocodile unexpectedly surfaces, you won't be able to outswim it, but if you can grab its jaws before it opens them, you'll have a chance of keeping its jaws shut (this assumes there's no part of your body between them). Yell for help.

3. If the crocodile has clamped its jaws on one of your limbs, try to reach for a stick or anything else to use as a weapon and hit its sensitive nose repeatedly and poke it in the eyes. (A man actually managed to make a crocodile let go of his arms by biting its nose as hard as he could.) It might just back off, but crocs are quick, and you'll have to keep fighting until you're safe. Carry on yelling.

4. As a last resort, play dead. Crocodiles shake their prey underwater to drown it but will stop when they think it's dead. Make your escape when it moves off.

HOW TO SWIM FREESTYLE

So you want to ditch the doggy paddle? The fastest and most impressive-looking swimming stroke is the freestyle (also called the front crawl).

Body and head. Your body should be straight and streamlined, with no arms and legs sticking out and your hips in line with your shoulders. Keep your face in the water, looking at the bottom of the pool. Only move your head when you need to take a breath. As you swim try to keep all of your body close to the surface of the water.

Legs. Use these to keep you up and maintain your balance as well as to propel you along. Try to make long, fast kicks, ensuring that the whole length of each leg is moving up and down. Bend your knees slightly and splash only a little with your feet. Try counting to six quickly and kicking your legs alternately in time with this.

It is important to keep your legs close together (but of course not so close that they move as one).

Arms. These are your main source of power. Stretch one arm in front of your head as far as you can, close to the surface of the water, letting your shoulders and hips follow. Then slice your hand down through the water, thumb first, splashing as little as possible. Keep your fingers together, forming a shallow scoop to help push through the water. As you bring your arm down, bend your elbow and push your hand towards your feet, your fingers following a path down the middle of your chest and stomach. When you bring the arm back up to repeat this stroke, try to lift your elbow out of the water first.

Keeping your hand near the water surface and close to your body, move it forward to the start position in front of your head.

The second arm should follow the first so that it is about to go down in front of you as the first is coming up. With some practise you'll slip into the rhythm of the alternating strokes, your hips and shoulders rolling slightly to the left or the right as you stretch each hand forward.

Breathing. Your face is in the water, so you must remember to turn your head when you want to take a breath. Turn it as smoothly as you can, leaving the side of your head resting in the water. An effective method is to turn your head to the left to breathe when your right arm is outstretched and to bring your head round to the right to breathe again as you stretch out your left arm.

You should now be able to kick, pull and breathe. Keep your legs kicking all of the time and your arms following each other. Get into the habit of breathing regularly, every two, three or four arm strokes. And try to avoid splashing too much – it's not cool or professional.

HOW TO PLAY A PIECE OF GRASS

1. Find the biggest piece of grass you can – the taller and wider the better.

2. Press the sides of your thumbs together, with the nails facing towards you.

3. Place the piece of grass between your thumbs, so that it runs from top to bottom.

4. You will now be able to see a strip of grass in the gap between your knuckles and where your thumbs meet your hands.

5. Blow through the gap. If you don't hear a whistle at first, adjust your lips and the grass, and keep trying.

HOW TO BE A VIP

If you are very important, you must know very important people. So impress your friends by greeting any stranger you pass by in the street who looks as though he or she might have some kind of status. Quite often the person will say 'Hello' back, thinking that you're the child of someone they know. 'Who's that?' your friends will ask. 'Oh, that's Lady So-and-so, an old friend of ours;' or 'That's Sir Henry. He owes me a favour – that's why he pretended not to see me. I'm going to have to call him;' or 'That was DJ Dingbat. He's always asking me what CDs to buy.' And so on. Don't overdo it – your friends will catch on. But get it right and they'll be full of respect.

HOW TO TIE THREE ESSENTIAL KNOTS

Different knots are used for different purposes. Here are three really useful knots that you can use all the time.

Reef knot. This is used to tie one rope to another if the ropes are of the same thickness. This knot is also useful for tying bandages, because it lies flat. When tying, always remember 'left over right and under, right over left and under'. When you have finished, pull the knot tight.

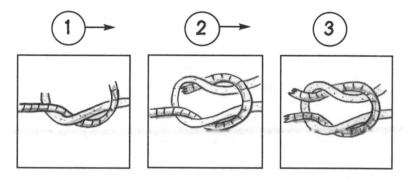

Sheet bend. If you need to tie two ropes together that are of different thicknesses you should use a sheet bend. When you have finished, pull the knot tight.

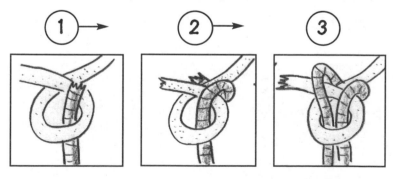

Clove hitch. This knot is used to tie a rope to an object. Sailors might use a clove hitch to tie their boats to a jetty.

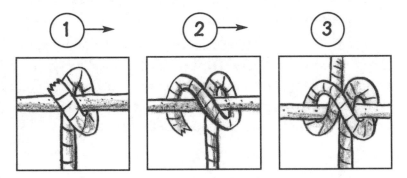

HOW TO AVOID BEING EATEN BY A POLAR BEAR

To avoid a polar bear in the wild, keep a clean camp. Bears can sniff food and rubbish smells from a long way away. Stay away from mammal carcasses. Never pet a polar bear cub.

If you are unlucky enough to be approached by a polar bear, stand your ground. Make yourself look bigger by holding a jacket over your head. Shout at the bear. If all else fails, throw the bear your sandwiches and run.

HOW TO PLAY THE TOILET ROLL

A kazoo is one of the world's simplest musical instruments. To make one you will need: a cardboard tube (from a roll of kitchen paper, clingfilm, foil or toilet roll), greaseproof paper, an elastic band, scissors, a ruler, a pencil, and coloured pens or paint.

1. Start by decorating your tube (this is optional, but who wants to be seen playing a toilet roll?).

2. That done, cut a square, 12x12cms (5x5ins), of greaseproof paper.

3. Place the greaseproof paper over one end of the tube and secure it with the elastic band.

4. Hum or sing into the open end. The greaseproof paper vibrates to give a buzzing effect that enhances the sound you make.

HOW TO SPOOK YOUR FAMILY

Could your house be haunted? It could be, if you have anything to do with it ...

Every morning, your family come downstairs to find that the table has been laid – and that one chair is pulled out, and there's tea in the cup at that place, as though someone had been sitting there and had just got up from the table moments before ... But there's no one there.

Things move. However often your mother puts that vase of flowers on the mantelpiece, the next time she comes into the room, it is back on the table. And that's not the only thing that moves. Furniture, too, appears to have moved by itself during the night.

The dog whines and scrabbles at the never-used door to the cellar (or spare room, broom cupboard, etc.). Nobody knows why – except you – you know his favourite chew toy is hidden behind it.

At night, when everybody is asleep, lights go on, found in the morning by whoever is first to get up. (Make sure no one hears you get up in the night.)

One particular door seems always to open by itself (the one to which you can attach a bit of thread without its being spotted).

Clothes that have been scattered about all appear neatly folded in a pile. Some clothes disappear from one drawer to reappear in someone else's drawer.

Other things seem to have moved. The tins in the cupboard are stacked, their labels swapped, and the eggs in the fridge are hard boiled. And the chocolate and biscuits keep disappearing!

Footsteps, music and talking are heard from another part of the house, but there's no one there. (Keep whatever machinery you use to record and play sounds well hidden.)

HOW TO MAKE A BALLOON SWORD

1. Get a long, skinny balloon and blow it up all the way.

2. Let a little air out and tie a knot at the end of the balloon.

3. Make a twist in the balloon about 10cm (4in) down from the knot and hold. This will be the handle. Don't let go or it will come apart.

4. Make two more twists about 8cm (3in) apart from each other, after the first twist. This will form half of the cross piece of the sword.

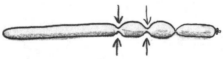

5. Twist the first and last twist together.

6. If you now twist this with the handle you can let go of it.

7. Make two more 8cm (3in) bubbles for the second part of the handle, just as before.

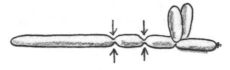

8. Twist the last twist around the first twist to secure the handle in place.

9. Make any adjustments you need and straighten out your sword.

HOW TO GIVE MOUTH-TO-MOUTH RESUSCITATION

Mouth-to-mouth resuscitation could save a person's life. Many types of injury can cause someone to stop breathing, and if this happens, a person has little time before they suffer brain damage or death. Don't practise on a person who is breathing – it can be dangerous, so use a doll.

1. Check to see if the casualty is breathing. If he's not, quickly check to see if there is any blockage in the air passages – including his tongue. Use your fingers to remove any obstruction you find. Call an ambulance.

2. Now check again as the removal of a blockage may have started him breathing again.

3. If not, put him on his back and loosen his clothing.

4. Tilt his head well back by lifting his chin. Hold him firmly by the chin and by the top of the head. Make sure his airway (the passage in the throat) is clear.

5. Hold his head and pinch his nostrils shut between your finger and thumb.

6. Take a deep breath, and then seal your lips firmly round his mouth. Breathe out steadily into his mouth. His chest should rise (if it doesn't it means there's a blockage to be removed – quickly). Remove your mouth, watch the chest fall, and then blow into his mouth again.

7. Check for breathing and check the pulse by placing your first two fingers on the underside of his wrist.

8. Continue the pattern of blowing into the casualty's mouth and watching his chest rise and fall for 12 breaths. Check again, and if he hasn't started breathing by himself continue until he does or until help arrives.

9. If he's started breathing, you'll need to put him in the recovery position. Place the arm closest to you straight out from the body. Lift and bend his far arm at the elbow, resting it against the near cheek. Grab and bend his far knee and then, protecting his head with one hand, gently roll him towards you by pulling his far knee over and to the ground. Stay close until help arrives.

HOW TO FOOL YOUR FRIENDS WITH TOOTHPICKS

Freak out your friends with this simple but sneaky trick.

1. Look carefully at this diagram. Arrange four square-ended toothpicks in exactly the same way.

2. Ask your friends to make a square by moving only one toothpick. They will really struggle.

3. Move the left-hand toothpick a little to the left and, in the middle of the toothpicks, a sneaky square will appear. It is important to have the blunt ends of the toothpicks in the middle of the square.

HOW TO EAT IN A POSH RESTAURANT

DO

Put your napkin on your knee straight away.

Start with the outer cutlery and work your way in with each course.

Finish your mouthful and wipe your mouth with your napkin before sipping water.

Say 'Excuse me' if you need to leave the table.

DON'T

Lean your elbows on the table.

Eat French fries with your fingers.

Eat with your mouth open.

Yell at the waiter.

Say 'Urghhhh!' if you don't like something.

HOW TO SERVE LIKE A WIMBLEDON CHAMPION

You have complete control of the shot as it starts with you. Keep calm and take the time to get into position. At all times, remember: balance, timing and rhythm.

1. Grip the racket, spreading your fingers around the handle without squeezing too hard. Keep your arm relaxed. Take the ball in the other hand.

2. Facing the net, point your racket at where you want the ball to go and use your throwing hand (this will be your left hand if you are right-handed) to support the ball lightly.

3. Raise your hands together just a short way, then bring them down together. As you do this start to turn your body so that you are sideways to the court. At the same time transfer your weight from your front foot to your back foot. Try to keep this sequence of movements smooth and co-ordinated.

4. Raise your throwing arm (left if you're playing right-handed) into an upright position to release the ball above your head. A good height to throw the ball is about 15cm (6ins) above your normal reach. Keep your arm straight to help throw the ball accurately

and make sure you don't release the ball too soon – it will fly at an angle towards the net and force you to lean forward to hit it.

5. While the ball is in the air you need to bring the racket fluidly back and up, ready to hit the ball. This is the most difficult part of the action, because at the same time as co-ordinating your arms you also need to transfer your weight from your back foot on to your front.

6. As the ball gets to the top of the throw, direct the racket at the ball in a swift throwing action. Aim to hit the ball at full stretch, with your racket arm straight, at the highest point you can reach it. The higher you make contact the more power you can generate and the harder and faster the ball will go.

7. Follow the motion through with your body, then look to recover quickly ready for your next shot.

HOW TO GET RID OF HICCUPS

Swallow a teaspoon of sugar,

or gulp down a glass of water,

or eat a piece of dry bread slowly,

or gargle water,

or drink water from the farthest side of the glass rim,

or hold your breath and count backwards,

or try all these at once – you'll probably feel so ill and confused that you'll forget about your hiccups.

HOW TO MUMMIFY AN ANCIENT EGYPTIAN

You are an ancient Egyptian, working as an embalmer. The family of a rich noblewoman who has recently died, come to you. They wish to preserve her body to make sure her soul has somewhere to reside during the afterlife.

1. First, using special custom-made hooks and spoons, you draw out the brain through the nose. This is very tricky, as you have to be careful not to damage the face.

2. You then take out the internal organs (the lungs, liver, stomach, intestines and so on) through a cut made in the left side of the tummy. The heart, however, you leave where it is.

3. Your helpers then wash the body in spiced palm wine.

4. When that's done, you cover the body, packing it inside as well as out (especially all round the heart), with natron, a mineral salt found in dried lake beds. You leave the natron there for 40 days to absorb all the moisture from the body. In the meantime you have been treating the removed organs in the same way. These used to be stored in special 'canopic' jars and buried alongside the mummy; you, however, use the new practice of preserving them, wrapping them up and popping them back into the body.

5. After 40 days, the body should be completely dried out, and look shrivelled and wrinkled. You clean away the natron and rub oils into the skin to soften it. You pad out the body with strong-smelling herbs and spices, mud, sawdust, rags and other bits of linen to stop it from sinking in and losing its shape. That done, you pop out the eyes and replace them with false ones.

6. Wrapping-up time can take many days as there are 20 layers of linen strips – hundreds of metres – to wind round the body. As you wind the bandages round the mummy you slip in various charms, made of precious metals and precious stones, among the linen strips. On some of the bandages you write prayers and magic words. You use resin glue to keep the bandages in place.

7. As your current customer is from a noble family, you have been asked to place a gold-leaf-covered mask over the almost fully bandaged head. (You made sure that the mask-maker managed a reasonable likeness of the dead noblewoman before you bound up the head.) Now you notice with approval that he has made her eyes bigger and nose smaller than they were in life – she might as well be more beautiful in the afterlife than she was in the life she has just left.

8. Your job is done, and you hand the mummy over to the specialist craftsmen who have been working on her coffin and tomb.

HOW TO RIP A PHONE DIRECTORY IN HALF

1. With the spine of the book towards you, place your hands on top of the book and grip it with your little and ring fingers. Bend the book into a U shape by pushing with your thumbs.

2. Now hold the book tightly with all your fingers and, while keeping the U shape in place, bend the book the other way so that the pages form a V shape.

3. As you continue to bend the edges of the book down, the pages will start to split.

4. Push with one of your hands and pull with the other to rip the book in half.

HOW TO PLAY POOHSTICKS

1. Find at least one other person to compete against.

2. Collect some sticks of all shapes and sizes.

3. Find a small footbridge over a stream.

4. Select a stick and compare it with those belonging to the other competitors to make sure you can tell them apart.

5. Stand side by side on the bridge facing upstream.

6. Secretly check for fast moving currents or slow, reedy areas and trapped logs.

7. On the count of three, drop your sticks into the water.

8. Quickly cross to the downstream side of the bridge and watch for the sticks to emerge.

9. The owner of the first stick to float out from under the bridge is the winner.

HOW TO WIN COMPUTER GAMES

It is a good idea to read the instruction manual and/or play the tutorial and pay attention to everything that happens in it. It is there to help you.

In shooting games:

- Snipe for preference (i.e. shoot from long distances with accurate, powerful guns).
- Aim for head shots.
- Zigzag and keep behind cover to avoid being sniped yourself.
- Remember to reload during quiet points, preferably behind cover.
- Use appropriate weapons – for instance, for assaults you need automatic firing and big clips.
- Be careful not to waste ammo – only use lots of bullets when you are surrounded by enemies.

In driving games, brake as you go round corners, and learn to use the handbrake.

In any games, if you know you're making the correct and only possible move, but it is apparently getting you nowhere, do persevere. It might be part of the game's programming that you have to make a certain number of attempts before you succeed.

Be alert at all times as you move through your game – watch out for anything that has moved or any object that you don't remember seeing last time you were in that location.

Collect anything that can be picked up – even the most unlikely items will probably come in useful.

If you're playing against one or more players in the same room, keep an eye on your opponent(s). Take your cue from what they are doing. And don't allow yourself to be distracted, either by external events, or by your opponents' comments.

Taunting your opponents often throws them completely off their game, giving you a chance to beat them: 'That tree/rock/hill looked really dangerous – lucky you got it in time!'; 'You have to expect corners'; 'Oh dear, dear. I didn't realize you were a beginner.' And so on.

Or 'advice' can put them off their game: 'Careful: look behind you.'; 'Ooh, I wouldn't do that, if I were you'; 'Look, you see that rock there?... Oh, too late. What bad luck.'

HOW TO SEE THROUGH YOUR HAND

1. Take a cardboard tube (from a roll of kitchen paper or toilet paper) and look through it with your right eye.

2. Place the edge of your left hand over the end of the tube with its palm facing you.

3. With both eyes open, stare at the point where the tube and the edge of your hand meet and you'll see that you have a hole in your hand.

HOW TO WRITE A QUICK POEM

A homework topic that usually provokes groans starts with the words, 'Write a poem about...' If the topic is boring it's even harder to be creative, but here is a quick, unfailing way to impress your teachers and be the envy of friends.

1. On line one, write the subject (say you've been told to write about a storm): 'Storm'.

2. On line two, write down two descriptive words that spring to your mind when you think of storms: 'Dark, angry'.

3. On line three, write three verbs (action words) connected to a storm: 'Blows, howls, crashes'.

4. On line four, write a thought that comes to you: 'Will it never end'.

5. On line five, write another phrase to describe the subject (i.e. storm): 'Nature's rage'.

6. Storm.

   Dark, angry,

   Blows, howls, crashes.

   Will it never end,

   Nature's rage?

OR: Me.

   Modest but wonderful,

   I can, I know and I do.

   The best at everything,

   That's me!

You will soon do much better than this. And then, if you like, you can refine your new skill – make it rhyme or add more lines as you want. Soon your friends will be coming to you for help in writing messages in greetings cards.

HOW TO GET OUT OF QUICKSAND

Whatever you do, don't think of all those films in which a character is gradually sucked, struggling and screaming, into the depths of the quicksand, then vanishes from sight with a faint plop. Remind yourself instead that you can float on quicksand – it is in fact a lot easier to float on quicksand than in water.

1. The worst thing to do is to thrash around and move your arms and legs through the mixture – you will only succeed in forcing yourself farther down into the quicksand.

2. If you are heading to an area where you think there may be quicksand, including riverbanks, beaches and marshes, carry a stout stick. If you find yourself sinking in quicksand lay the stick down on the surface of the quicksand and gently slide onto it on your back. Your body weight will spread out across the stick and you will find it easier to float. If you don't have a stick, turn onto your back and slowly spread out your arms and legs to increase your surface area.

3. Once afloat, move very slowly and carefully using your arms, and edge your way towards firm ground.

HOW TO MAKE A SIMPLE RAFT

You will need: four straight wooden poles, about 182cm (6ft) long and 8–10cm (3–4ins) thick; three shorter wooden poles of the same thickness, but about 122cm (4ft) long; at least 61m (200ft) of 5-mm ($^3/_{16}$-in) thick nylon cord; at least 12 strong 5-litre (1.1-gallon; 1.3 US gallons) empty rectangular plastic containers of the kind used for detergent (caps should be screwed on tight); any planks or boards, at least 182cm (6ft) long, that you can find; nails, hammer, screwdriver, and scissors or a knife.

1. Lay the end of one of the shorter poles over the end of a longer one and at right angles to it, and lash them together with the nylon cord. Lay the other end of the shorter pole over the end of a second longer one, and lash together; then lash the free ends of the two longer poles under each end of a second shorter one – creating a rectangular structure.

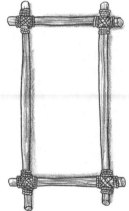

2. Lash each end of the third shorter pole across and over the middle of the two longer ones; then lash the third and fourth long poles beneath the middle of the three shorter crossways poles – the distance between these two long poles should be just wider than the narrowest side of one of the empty containers. You should now have a rectangle consisting of four long poles crossed by three shorter ones laid on top of them.

3. Now lash three of the empty 5-litre containers at even intervals along the outside of one of the outer long poles, the caps pointing towards the stern (rear) of the raft. Repeat along the outside of the other outer long pole, and then again between the two centre long poles.

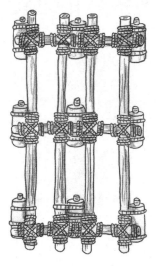

4. Launch the raft in shallow water and test its buoyancy – ideally, deck level should be about 15cm (6ins) above the surface of the water when a person is sitting on the raft. If necessary, lash more containers to the long poles (you can get six containers along each pole) until you achieve the right degree of buoyancy. But remember to allow for the fact that you will be adding more weight when you fix the decking, which will make the raft sit lower in the water.

5. Now fix your decking of boards or planks to the three shorter cross poles – lash them in place, or otherwise nail or screw them to the cross poles. There can be gaps between the deck planks – in fact, the lighter you build your raft, the better it will float. The decking planks don't need to touch each other.

6. Relaunch the raft and climb aboard.

A useful knot for putting together a raft is the square lashing. Find out how to do it in a knot book or on the Internet.

HOW TO MAKE A STINK

Other than the most obvious way, that is ...

Although you can buy traditional stink bombs you can make something that smells just as bad very cheaply and easily.

You will need: an egg, a drop of milk, half a teaspoon of sugar and a tin or plastic food container with a lid that can be shut tight. If plastic, it ought to be made of bendy rather than rigid plastic, which could crack with the pressure of the noxious gas.

1. Break the egg into the container, add the milk and sugar and shut your container tight. Put it in a warm place, preferably outdoors – somewhere that gets a lot of sun. If it has to be indoors, hide it near a boiler or radiator. Leave it for about two weeks.

2. After two weeks use a suitable instrument to make about 20 holes in the lid of the container.

3. Now find a good place to hide your creation. Soon a delightful stink will be wafting out, and you can enjoy watching everyone wandering about sniffing and looking for the source of the revolting smell.

Top tip. It is best to avoid letting stink bombs off at school. Your teachers will not be impressed that you are the best at making them.

HOW TO TEACH A PARAKEET TO TALK

To ensure you have a bird with the ability to talk, and one that you can train, choose a young male Australian parakeet, or an English, Ringnecked, Alexandrine or Plumheaded parakeet.

Parakeets develop their communication skills by talking to each other, so if you can, keep two or three birds. If not, a useful trick is to put a mirror in your bird's cage. This will cheer him up and he will chat happily with his own reflection just as if it were another bird in the cage. Be sure to remove the mirror when you start teaching the parakeet to talk – or he may prefer to talk to himself.

To train your bird, first you must make friends with him – spend time with him, talk to him, keep his cage clean, give him plenty of clean water and make sure he is well fed.

Train him to sit on your hand or finger.

To teach him to talk, speak clearly and slowly, repeating the word or phrase over and over. Parakeets tend to speed up words when they repeat them, so speak slowly and your parakeet will pronounce the word correctly.

Parakeets can recognize and pick up certain sounds better than others.

They are best with consonants such as d, k, t, p or b. A traditional phrase such as 'Hello, how are you?' isn't very good to start with, since it is hard for the bird to say.

It is important to speak to your parakeet regularly and to speak to him for more than a few minutes – if possible make your training session at least half an hour a day.

During lessons, cover the top and three sides of his cage with a towel or cloth, so that he is not distracted from you or your voice.

Don't move on to a second word or phrase until he can repeat the first one. Be patient; once he has learnt a few words, it will take much less time to learn more.

Once a parakeet learns to repeat words, you can teach him to recognize an object and say its name, like a book or pen. Simply hold the object up to the bird and repeat the word.

After a while you can train your bird to recognize you by your name (or whatever you choose to call yourself). 'Good morning, Boss.' your bird might greet you. But be careful not to refer to any of your family members by nicknames you would prefer to keep secret in front of your new talkative pet.

HOW TO HOOT WITH YOUR HANDS

1. Use your hands to form a cave with only one entrance, the slit between your thumbs. There are two ways for you to make this cave:

a) Clasp your hands together with the fingers of one hand (A) folded over the other between the thumb and first finger, and the fingers of the other hand (B) folded over the outside of hand A. Hand A's thumb rests lightly on hand B's. Now adjust your hands to form a cave between them, with the two outer edges of your hands right against each other. Make sure there are no gaps between the edges of your hands or any of your fingers, and make sure that the wrist edges of your hands are pressed together.

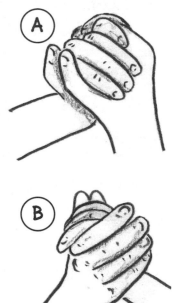

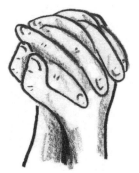

b) Instead of clasping your hands together, lace your fingers tightly together so there are no gaps for air to get through. Make sure the wrist edges of your hands are pressed tightly and then pull your palms away from each other, so as to form your cave.

2. For either kind of cave, relax your thumbs so that they are slightly bent, with the side of the nails touching. Line up the upper part of your thumbs with the underside of your first finger. You will now have a slit – wider in the middle than the top or bottom – between your thumbs.

3. Place your lips on your thumb knuckles, the upper lip resting on the bases of your thumbnails and the bottom lip resting just below your knuckles. Be very careful not to close the air hole with your lower lip – the air that you are about to blow into your cave needs to come out.

4. Blow steadily – and not too hard – through your knuckles. If you're lucky you'll hear a raspy almost-hoot (if you're very lucky you might hear a kind of whistly hoot); if you're not so lucky you'll just hear a puffing sound.

Adjust your fingers and thumbs carefully, make sure your cave is still sealed tight, and that the air that you are blowing through the top of the air hole is coming out through the bottom (you can probably feel it coming out). It can help to have damp, even wet, hands.

5. Keep trying. Sooner or later you will get a good hoot and, as you practise, it will become easier and the sound will become clearer. Then you can start experimenting with blowing harder or softer, bending and flexing your fingers and thumbs, squeezing your hands together, etc., to change the note.

HOW TO SPEAK IN CODE

Eggy-peggy: Add 'egg' before each vowel.
Example: 'Eggi eggam thegge beggest.' ('I am the best.')

Gree: Add 'gree' to the end of every word.
Example: 'Igree amgree thegree bestgree.'

Na: Add 'na' to the end of every word.
Example: 'Ina amna thena bestna.'

Pig latin: Move the first letter to the end of the word and add 'ay' to it.
Example: 'Iay maay hetay estbay.'

HOW TO MAKE A BALLOON DOG

1. Blow up a long, skinny balloon, leaving 3cm (1¼ins) of unblown balloon at the end.

2. Tie a knot at the end of the balloon.

3. Make a twist in the balloon about 5cm (2ins) from the knotted end.

4. Make two more twists about 2¹/₂cm (1in) apart from each other, after the first twist. Make sure not to let go of the balloon.

5. Twist the two smaller bubbles together. These will become the ears. You will see that you have already made the dog's head.

6. Make three more twists about 5cm (2ins) apart and twist these sections together. These will be the neck and the two front legs.

7. Now, make three more twists, one for the dog's body, and two more about 5cm (2ins) apart for its back legs.

8. Fold and twist the two smaller sections together and twist the legs down. Use a felt-tip pen to draw on eyes and a mouth if you like.

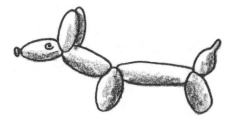

HOW TO BUILD A CAMPFIRE

You never know when you will need to keep warm in the great outdoors and it is essential to know how to make a safe, successful campfire.

1. Make sure you have the permission of the person who owns the land. Choose a suitable spot – away from anything that might catch fire, especially trees, bushes and buildings. Make sure that your belongings are out of the way and remove stones from the area, as these can get very hot and shatter explosively. It is a good idea to have a bucket of water or sand (or soil) close by in case your fire gets too enthusiastic.

2. If the site for the fire is grassy, cut around and under a 1m (3¹/₄ft) square of turf. Lift it out, lay it right side up and sprinkle it with water. The grass should stay fresh until you replace it after you have broken camp. Make your fire in the space from which you lifted the turf.

3. You will need three kinds of burnable material: tinder, kindling and fuel. Tinder is light stuff that catches fire easily – like shredded bark, dry grass or dry pine needles. Gather enough to half-fill a standard-size bucket. Kindling is slim, dry dead twigs – no thicker than a pencil. Collect at least enough to fill the same bucket.

4. For fuel you will need firewood – dead, dry sticks thicker than kindling. Start by filling your bucket – you can collect more fuel as and when necessary. Make sure your fuel is neither green nor wet, as this will make the fire smoke.

5. Make a heap of the tinder, then lean the kindling over it to build a triangular structure like a tepee; over this place some of the firewood, also standing and leaning in. Too much fuel will stifle your fire – there should be plenty of air space beneath the kindling and fuel.

6. Light the tinder. If it takes, the kindling will catch fire too and as it burns more strongly the firewood should take.

7. You will soon have a merry little fire. But keep an eye on it – fire is sneaky. And when you have finished, make sure you put the fire out completely – not a single glowing ember should be left. Spread the ashes out, and pour on some water to be on the safe side. Replace the turf you removed.

HOW TO BECOME A CATHOLIC SAINT

1. Die. In the Roman Catholic church, you cannot usually become a saint until at least five years after your death.

2. Local bishops must investigate your life, and send their findings to the Pope.

3. The Pope proclaims you are a virtuous role model.

4. Two verifiable miracles must have occurred because of you. (Officially, a miracle must involve no trickery and must also suspend the laws of nature.)

HOW TO TIE A TIE

Lift up your shirt collar and put the tie round your neck so that both ends hang down at the front. The wide end should hang about 30cms (1ft) lower than the thin end.

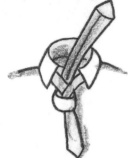

1. Cross the wide end over the thin end near the collar, then take it round underneath the thin end.

2. Bring the wide end over the thin end again and back underneath. Push it up through the back of the V-shape made by the partially formed knot.

3. Bring the wide end forward (i.e. away from you) through the V and down through the front loop of the knot.

4. Hold the thin end and slide the knot up to your neck. Hold the knot and with the other hand pull on each end of the tie until the knot is tight.

HOW TO ANNOY YOUR BROTHERS AND SISTERS

With these tricks, your brothers and sisters will be so annoyed they'll be irritated just having you in the room. But beware of the consequences – don't do any of these things unless you're prepared for war.

Hang around when your brother or sister is lounging in front of the telly and, when you hear your parents approaching, quickly busy yourself tidying the room – you'll get endless praise from your parents, whilst your sibling will be frowned upon for his or her laziness. To keep yourself amused while you wait for your parents to see you working so hard, find as many excuses as possible for walking slowly past the TV screen and blocking your brother's or sister's view.

Tie a knot in one of your brother's pyjama legs. Do it on random nights so he never expects it, and always falls over with a thud.

If your brother or sister has the traditional two sheets and a bedspread or blanket on their bed, make an apple-pie bed (make sure you are around to see them get into bed). To do this, pull off the bedspread/blanket and tuck in the head end of the top sheet at the head of the bed, and cover it with the pillow. Then untuck the bottom end of the top sheet and fold it upwards so that it goes up to, and preferably slightly over, the pillows. Tidy all the folds and cover it with the bedspread so that it looks exactly as it always does.

If your brother or sister has a girlfriend or boyfriend, it's just too good an opportunity to miss: leave humiliating photos of them lying around throughout the house; bring up the subject of your many farting competitions over dinner; if there's an extension phone make burping sounds down the line when they talk to each other.

When your brother or sister is about to go out, make sure that whatever is most vital to him or her is missing. After ten minutes of furious searching, you will 'find' it; the first time

you might be met with thanks, but your brother or sister will soon catch on and get very annoyed.

Get a TV guide and look up what is on at the same time as the soaps your sister watches every night, then tell your parents that you need to watch something on the other channel for school. Act totally bored by the programme whenever your parents are out of sight.

When you do homework together claim to need everything that they are using, the calculator, the ruler etc. Whilst you wait to 'use' these items, drum on the table, or hum to

yourself. When they finally give up the item find something pointless to do with it – use the calculator to write the word 'shell' upside down (77345), and the ruler to underline your name on your notebook.

HOW TO TAKE A PENALTY KICK

You have three things to consider: the goalkeeper, how you kick the ball, and where you send the ball.

1. **Goalkeeper**. The goalie's aim is first of all to distract you and put you off your kick. Check the goalie's position but don't pay him any other attention. If you look at the goalie, he's gained an advantage.

The goalie's second aim is to save the penalty, either by predicting which way you'll kick the ball or by waiting, following and stopping the ball.

2. **Ball**. There are two favoured techniques for kicking the ball. One is to kick the ball hard with the laces of your boot – the advantage is that it's a powerful shot; the disadvantage is that there is more risk of the ball going wide or straight over the crossbar. The second technique is to kick the ball with the side of the foot, with less power but more accuracy.

3. **Aim**. Before kicking, select the spot where you wish to direct the ball, but do not look at this position and risk giving it away to the goalie. You might want to try tricking the goalie by approaching the ball as if you're going to kick it in one direction, but then kick it the other way, or by running up to the ball as though you are about to hit it hard with the laces of your boot, but instead use the side of your foot to place the ball to the right or the left. The best odds are to aim high and preferably to the left or right, as a low centre shot stands less chance of getting past the goalie.

HOW TO HYPNOTIZE A CHICKEN

Rest assured that no chicken is hurt during this, not even its dignity is shaken (unless you can ask it to run around like a human when it is in the trance). This is one of several ways to lull a chicken into a stupor – just make sure you are gentle and quiet.

1. Place the chicken on a table, laying it on its side with one wing under its body. Hold it down gently with its head flat on the surface.

2. With one finger from your free hand repeatedly trace a straight line, about 30cm (1ft) long, in front of the bird's eyes – outwards from its beak-tip and along the table. Alternatively, take a piece of chalk (a colour that contrasts with the surface) and draw a 30-cm (1-ft) line from the beak-tip out in front of the bird. Hold the chicken still for a bit as it stares ahead along the line.

Soon it will be in a hypnotic trance. How long it remains in that trance varies from seconds to hours. But any sudden movement or noise will bring the bird to and with a squawk of surprise it'll be up and off and on its way.

HOW TO TREAT STINGS

You can recognize if a person is allergic to a sting if they have difficulty breathing, their pulse speeds up, they collapse, or areas of the body away from the site of the sting swell up. If you see any of these signs, be sure immediately to call an ambulance, but also ask the person if they've got treatment with them (some carry adrenalin ready to be injected). Likewise if they've been very badly stung or have been stung in the mouth or eyes, call an ambulance at once.

Otherwise, when a person is stung, they will suffer only short-lived pain and some discomfort that can be soothed by pressing something cool on to the affected area or rubbing it with an ice cube.

Bee stings. Carefully pull out the sting with tweezers, gripping the sting where it's closest to the skin. To soothe the pain, dab the sore patch with a solution of bicarbonate of soda. Fresh wee also soothes ... yuck!

Wasp stings. Wasps don't leave their sting behind. If you dab vinegar on the stung area, it will reduce the pain.

Jellyfish stings. These are painful but usually harmless (the dangerous one is the Portuguese Man-of-War, recognized by its blue-mauve bladder that floats on the surface). Rinse the sore area thoroughly. Calamine lotion will soothe it.

Nettle stings. Rubbing with dock leaves (a green-leaved weed with clusters of small greenish or reddish petal-less flowers) provides the best relief. If you can't find dock leaves try mint (recognizable by its scent).

HOW TO CLIMB A PALM TREE

You need to be barefoot to get a grip on the tree, but wear a long-sleeved shirt and trousers to protect yourself from a bad scraping.

Climb like a frog. Flex your legs on each side of the tree with the soles of your feet firmly against the sides of the trunk. Your legs should look like those of a frog, bent knees sticking out either side of you. Move one hand up, against the other side of the trunk and place the other hand at chest level on your side of the tree. Move yourself up by straightening your legs, shifting your weight to your hands and, with a jump-like motion, bringing up both of your feet at the same time to return to the frog position, progressing up the tree as you do so. Rest after each few 'jumps'.

When you can reach the palm leaves, grab hold and make your way up to the coconuts.

Going down. Either return to the frog-like position, feet first, and jump down step-by-step, or lower your hands one by one behind the trunk while allowing the soles of your feet to slide down against the trunk.

HOW TO BE FIRST OFF THE STARTING BLOCKS

1. As you wait for the starter's commands, breathe gently and try to relax – to help your body run efficiently and quickly.

2. **'On your marks.'** Crouch on one knee and place your hands just behind the starting line, forming a high bridge between your fingers and thumbs. Your hands should be placed slightly further apart than your shoulders. Keep your eyes fixed on the ground ahead of you to help your balance, focus and relaxation. Try not to allow anything to distract you.

3. **'Set.'** Raise your hips so they're just higher than your shoulders. Keep your head at a comfortable angle – don't try to look up at the track but don't look right down either. Lean your body as far forward as you can and aim to begin running without stumbling. Breathe in. Be ready for the starting signal.

4. **'Go.'** Breathe out hard and pump your arms and legs. To start with try not to take too big strides, wait until you're balanced and are running rhythmically. Thrust your elbows as high as possible with each backward swing and drive your legs with a high knee action.

5. Keep going, and leave everyone else behind.

HOW TO PLAY A TRICK ON THE WHOLE CLASS

Before you play your trick, enlist a partner in crime, explain how the trick works and prepare a keyword to use that only the two of you know about.

1. Announce to your class that you have telepathic powers. To prove your point, you will leave the room while the class, or a single volunteer, chooses an object from the room and tells your partner what it is.

2. When you return, your partner will ask you what object the volunteer is thinking of – 'Could it be the lamp?', 'Is it the window?', 'Or is it the green plant?'. Consider each of these questions, as though connecting with your powers, but to each one answer 'No.'

3. Then your partner asks, 'Is it the red chair?' You answer 'No,' but they have alerted you with the word 'red'. This is the keyword that you have chosen, and when your partner uses this keyword you know that the next question they ask will be the right answer. 'Is it the picture on the wall?' your partner asks next, to which you reply, 'Yes.' 'It was.' gasps the astonished class. And you take your bow.

4. Pick five or six keywords and alternate between them ('red', 'big', 'on the table' etc.). Or use signals such as the way your partner points or the way you enter the room – putting three fingers round the edge of the door could signal to your partner to say the correct object on his third question. Your class will never be able to spot how the trick works and your answers will always be correct.

HOW TO VANQUISH A VAMPIRE

So you have suspicions about your neighbour, the one who never seems to come out during the day. He is tall, thin and pale, with smoothly combed black hair. He has a whispery voice, with a foreign accent, and when he speaks he covers his teeth. Could he have something to hide? You had better do some checking.

1. Choose a bright sunny day to approach his house, scatter garlic bulbs around his front door then retreat to a safe hiding place. Wait until he comes out, and then watch his reaction. If he looks startled and heads rapidly back indoors, you might be on to something.

2. Return to his house with a large mirror. Stand in a hidden spot where you can see his front door reflected in

the mirror. When the door opens, can you see him in the mirror? If he has no reflection, he could be a vampire.

3. If all signs point to him being a vampire, you must take action. Arm yourself with lots more garlic, a crucifix, a sharpened wooden stake, and a bottle of holy water (if you have a spray bottle so much the better). Finally, collect a small group of carefully chosen helpers, who should be similarly armed.

4. With your trusty companions, make your way in daylight into the vampire's basement and find his coffin. Be prepared in case a werewolf or other monstrous creature comes out from the shadows to defend his master.

5. The vampire wakes up and rises from his coffin, showing his fangs, trying to get them into your neck.

6. You and your friends surround him. You are so well supplied with garlic and other vampire deterrents that he is weakening rapidly. As the vampire cowers, it is time for you to strike.

7. Hold your stake firmly in your hands, aim for where the vampire's heart would be if he had one, and plunge! The vampire crumbles into dust before your eyes.

Be sure to test your vampire before you send him into eternal darkness – chances are he's just a quiet man with bad teeth!

HOW TO WRITE A SECRET MESSAGE

All top secrets are best kept and passed in code. Devising your own code to use with a friend is the best way of ensuring no one will crack it:

1. Break your message into groups of two letters:

I AM THE BEST AT EVERYTHING
IA MT HE BE ST AT EV ER YT HI NG

2. Then reverse the letters in each pair:

AI TM EH EB TS TA VE RE TY IH GN

3. Now run the letters together:

AITMEHEBTSTAVERETYIHGN

Think about how you could adapt this code: adding a dummy letter between each pair of letters, swapping adjacent pairs, or reversing every other pair.

HOW TO READ A COMPASS

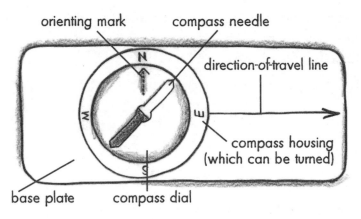

orienting mark   compass needle

direction-of-travel line

compass housing
(which can be turned)

base plate   compass dial

1. Hold the compass flat in front of you so as to allow the compass needle to float freely. Assuming there is nothing magnetic close by, the needle will point to magnetic north. (Do make sure there's nothing magnetic about, though – if, for instance, you had a magnet in your pocket the needle would point to that instead of to the north. Large metal objects – an iron gate, for instance – can also affect magnetic compasses.)

2. Rotate the compass housing until the orienting mark – N (for north) or the 0° symbol – lines up with the needle, making sure that it is the north end of the needle (indicated by a distinguishing mark – say by its being red) and not the south end hovering above the N or 0° mark.

3. Now you know where the magnetic north lies, which means that you now also know where south, east, west and all the other compass points are.

4. To use the compass to find your way to, say, a distant hill, aim the base plate of the compass so that the direction-of-travel line points exactly at the hill.

5. Turn the compass housing until the orienting mark is beneath the north end of the compass needle, then double-check to make sure that the direction-of-travel line is still pointing at the hill. You now have your bearings – and if you have taken them accurately, by following the direction-of-travel line while keeping the compass needle over the orienting mark, you will reach the hill.

HOW TO FALL WITHOUT HURTING YOURSELF ... MUCH

1. Try to relax and not fight the fall – unless it is clear that falling would lead to serious injury (e.g. if there are unfriendly hazards like rocks or heavy machinery), in which case try to send your body the other way.

2. Try not to land hands down as you could injure your wrists, elbows or shoulders.

3. Attempt to fall on your side rather than your front or back. Half-turn or roll if necessary to land on the fleshier parts of your body.

4. Don't allow your body to open out. Tuck up instead – chin firmly against chest, arms bent at the elbows to protect your head and face.

5. If you're on a bicycle, let go of it, try to swing your leg from under the bike and push the bike away from you.

HOW TO DO A WHEELIE

Impress your mates with this amazing bit of stunt riding.
A wheelie is difficult to perform on a road bike. It is easier
on a BMX-style bike because of the lower centre of gravity.

1. Sit on the bike.

2. Start pedalling until you get to about 8kph (5mph).

3. Stand on the pedals.

4. Lean back over the rear wheel.

5. Pull sharply on the handlebar while still pedalling.

6. As the front wheel rises, balance your weight and your
pedalling to maintain the wheelie.

Top tip. Keep your wheel at a good height and be careful
not to flip over on to your back – touching the back brake
will help prevent this.

HOW TO TAKE THE BEST PHOTOS

1. The most interesting photos capture a moment that might never happen again. As such moments can rarely be planned, try to keep your camera within easy reach.

2. When taking a photo of a person or animal, try to get a feeling of life and immediacy by establishing eye contact – or rather eye-to-lens contact.

3. Manual focusing can produce excellent results but quite often things change while you're still fiddling and the moment is lost. Automatic focusing is quicker but will assume that the object in the middle of the frame is what you wish to have in focus – what's behind, in front and to the sides will not come out as sharply. You might be able to lock the focus. To do this: you first centre the subject of your picture in the frame and then press and hold the shutter button halfway down. Then, still holding the shutter halfway down, you change the position of your camera so the subject is framed how you want it to be. Then press the shutter button to take the picture.

4. Some cameras have an automatic flash – this can be annoying if you are trying for an artistic shot using low-level lighting. Again, it might be possible to override the automatic flash. With many, though, the flash is manual – so remember to set it when it is needed.

Avoid taking photos too close up with a flash as the subject will appear bleached. The other common flash problem is 'red eye' in which the light is reflected off the back of the subject's eye. Some cameras have a red-eye reduction feature (with two flashes, the first to make the pupils smaller, the second to light up the subject). If yours does not, you could try flashing a bright light in your subject's face just before pressing the shutter (warn them first, though).

5. Visualize your photos as a whole. Look at the surrounding area – rather than just your subject. Choose your location carefully, check the background, remove or add items if necessary. Adjust lighting (there might be bright sun pouring through the window straight into your lens, or too little light).

6. Note that the morning or evening sun gives the most attractive light – in the middle of the day it can be too glaring. If you are taking a photograph in sunshine, be sure that the sun does not fall upon your lens. You might find that sunlight takes colour and definition from a subject's face – or exaggerates certain features.

7. With landscape, lighting is perhaps even more important than the location – in soft dawn light a view of a river curving through a field is beautiful, in the noonday sun it is flat and glaring, in the light of a sunset it is dramatic.

8. Experiment with taking photos from different angles. You do not have to be standing at eye-level – kneel down, or climb up on something to find the best perspective.

9. As always, practise is the key. For this reason a digital camera is probably the best as you can see and keep or reject your photos instantly.

HOW TO TIE A KNOT WITHOUT LETTING GO OF THE ENDS

1. Lay the piece of string in front of you and cross your arms so that one hand is over the other arm and one hand is under.

2. Keeping your arms folded, pick up each end of the string.

3. Keeping hold of the two ends, uncross your arms.

4. Ta-da! The string is tied in a knot.

HOW TO SURVIVE A VOLCANIC ERUPTION

First of all, know what you are up against. Deep down below the surface of the earth, a build-up of gases and the movement of the crustal plates increase pressure to a point where it can no longer be contained. The result is an explosion of boiling magma (molten rock) in the form of lava, flaming gases and red-hot fragments of rock and dust. Pretty scary stuff.

At any given time there are usually at least 12 volcanoes erupting somewhere in the world. If you find yourself living near one make sure you are prepared.

Stock up on provisions of bottled water, food, medical supplies, blankets, warm clothing and batteries in case power lines are cut. Collect water in your bath, sinks and containers as mains supplies may quickly become polluted.

In the event of an eruption, seek shelter at home and don't leave unless advised to by the authorities. Keep listening to the radio or TV for news and advice.

If you go outside, wear a mask and goggles to keep volcanic ash out of your eyes and lungs. Keep gutters and roofs clear of settling ash, which could bring down the house upon you.

If possible, don't accidentally wander away from other people, and always remain on the trodden paths.

If you are caught outside during an eruption, be aware of the hazards that come with an eruption: the flying debris, hot gases, lava flows, explosions, mudslides, avalanches, boiling water sprays from geysers, and floods. If you are in an area that could experience a lava flow, be ready to outrun it and never try to cross it.

Look for hills and head towards them. They may afford you some protection from the destructive and devastating effects of the eruption.

HOW TO JUGGLE

Take one ball and throw it from hand to hand. Make sure each throw goes straight up and to the same height (to about eye level). Catch the ball at waist level.

Now move on to two balls, one in each hand. Throw the first ball, A, as described above. Wait until it is about to descend and then throw the second ball, B, up underneath the first. If you can't react quickly enough at first, try throwing the balls higher to give yourself more time to catch them. If you find the balls are going forwards, throw them slightly in, towards yourself.

Continue practising with the two balls until you feel confident. Then practise starting with your second hand.

Repeat these moves, throwing the balls higher as you grow more confident. Always have at least one ball in the air, and never more than one in either hand. Watch the balls as they reach their highest point and don't reach up to them, let them come down to you.

Now try juggling with three balls. Here's how:

1. In your left hand hold ball A between your thumb, first and middle fingers, and ball C between your ring, little finger and your thumb. Ball B is in your right hand.

2. Throw ball A up; when it reaches its highest point, throw ball B. Catch ball A in your right hand.

3. When ball B reaches its highest point, throw ball C. Catch ball B in your left hand.

4. When ball C is at its highest point, throw ball A. Catch ball C. Throw ball B up and so on.

HOW TO READ SOMEONE'S MIND

Ask a friend to pick a number between 1 and 5. Ask them to multiply that number by 9. Ask them to add the digits of the number they get. Now ask them to subtract 5 from their answer.

Tell your friend to think of the letter in the alphabet that corresponds to their number (1 is A, 2 is B and so on). Tell them to think of a country in Europe that starts with that letter. Now ask them to think of an animal that starts with the last letter of that country. And then a colour that starts with the last letter of their animal. Now tell them that you know what they are thinking, and that it is an orange kangaroo in Denmark. Chances are that you're right.

HOW TO SAVE THE WORLD

1. Walk or cycle to school instead of being driven.

2. Save electricity by switching off appliances when you are not using them.

3. Recycle everything you can – either by reusing items for other purposes or by taking them to recycling banks.

4. Take an interest in environmental issues: on television, in newspapers and on the Internet.

5. Take out reusable bags when shopping, and refuse new ones when offered.

6. Take quick showers instead of deep baths.

7. Use energy-efficient light bulbs.

HOW TO MAKE A SQUEALER

The high-pitched squeal that some young animals make when in need will attract their mother as well as predators and other merely curious animals. You can make a device that imitates this squeal out of a hazel twig. Use it to see what animals you can attract.

You will need: one straight length of dry hazel twig about 2cm (³/₄in) thick and 16cm (6ins) long, a pocket knife with a strong sharp blade, three strong rubber bands – one of which must be approximately 9cm (3¹/₂ins) long and 4.5mm (³/₁₆in) wide unstretched.

1. Trim the ends of the hazel twig and cut off any minor twiglets and bumps.

2. With the knife (mind your fingers), split the twig lengthways into halves. To do this, stand the twig on one end and rest the blade of the knife across the other end so as to bisect it. Press down on the knife blade until it has started to cut. Then, holding the knife handle, tap the end of the blade repeatedly with a piece of wood to move it down through the twig.

3. Take one half of the twig and mark its centre. Then with the knife cut across the width of the twig half at two points, each about 2cm (³/₄in) from the marked centre,

to a depth of about $1^1/_2$mm ($^1/_{16}$in). Using the knife, carefully scrape out the wood between the two cuts. You should now have one half of the twig with a shallow dip, 4cm ($1^1/_2$ins) long, across its centre.

4. Repeat with the other half of the twig, making sure that the two ends of each half-twig match, so that they will fit together again.

5. Take the longer rubber band and stretch it lengthways along one half of the twig, so that it lies flat and runs over the centre of the dip in the middle. Then place the two halves of the twig back together, trapping the long rubber band running between them.

6. Bind each end of the twig with one of the other shorter rubber bands, making as many turns as necessary to keep the twig halves firmly together.

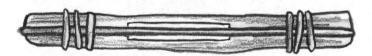

7. Hold the twig across your mouth with your lips over the dip in the centre. Blow gently. Provided the rubber band trapped in the dip is tight enough, the effect should be a loud high-pitched squeaking sound, caused by the air passing over the stretched rubber band. You can experiment with variations of the note by adjusting the tension of the long rubber band: tighter = higher pitched; looser = lower pitched.

8. Blow for about two to four seconds; the harder you blow the louder and, to a limited extent, the higher the pitch; ending the call with a short hard blast will produce a high-pitched squeal, as though a young animal was in immediate danger.

9. Conceal yourself in a hedge, ditch etc. Blow your squealer. In this way, depending on where you are, you might attract roe deer, rabbits, foxes, badgers, hedgehogs, local cats and dogs – as well as curious or annoyed neighbours.

HOW TO REPAIR A BICYCLE PUNCTURE

1. You'll need a puncture-repair kit, the bike manual and any necessary tools. Check the tyre for obvious causes of the flat – e.g. a nail or piece of glass. Unscrew the valve to let any remaining air out of the tube. Remove the tyre from the wheel carefully so as not to pinch the tube. Pull the tube out, pressing the valve through the hole in the rim (if it is secured with a rim nut, unscrew that first).

2. Look for the puncture. If it is not obvious, replace the valve, pump the tube up a little and listen for the hiss of escaping air, or dunk it in water. A stream of bubbles will reveal the site of the puncture.

3. Once you've found the puncture draw a circle round it. Making sure that the tube is completely dry, then lightly roughen the area round the puncture with fine sandpaper. This will allow the glue to bond better – don't be tempted to skip this step.

4. Apply a thin coat of rubber solution over the area where the leak is, covering an area slightly larger than the patch. Allow it to dry completely – three to five minutes (be patient) – if you don't, the patch will probably come off.

5. Take a patch of the right size and put a tiny blob of solution on its contact surface, then at once wipe off with your finger all but a very thin coat. Wait another three to five minutes. Then apply the patch, with the centre over the puncture, in one go (don't try to pull it off and reposition it), smoothing it down to get rid of any air bubbles. Press firmly.

6. Keep pressing it down really hard for at least a minute, especially round the edges. Wait for a couple of minutes and then carefully peel the backing paper or plastic off the patch. If an edge of the patch lifts with it, quickly press it back down; then try lifting the backing again from the other side. If the whole patch comes away with the backing, you'll have to start again with a new patch. (Self-adhesive patches do exist – but they do not always work very well.)

7. Once you've removed the backing, press down on the patch to seal the edges – then it's time to replace the inner tube. Dust it with French chalk (from your puncture repair kit – grate it on your sandpaper), especially all round the patch so it doesn't stick to the inside of the tyre. That done, replace the valve and pump a little air into the tube; this makes it easier to replace.

8. As you replace the tube, make sure the valve stem is correctly positioned and that the tube is not pinched or creased. If everything looks okay then pump the tyre up to normal pressure. Inflate the tyre to the correct pressure. You've done it – but keep an eye on the tyre for a while.

HOW TO MAKE A WATERBOMB

Start with a square piece of paper.

1. Fold in half across the middle in both directions, then unfold.

2. Turn over. Fold in half from corner to corner in both directions, then unfold.

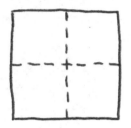

3. Fold along creases.

4. Fold corner to corner. Repeat behind.

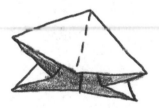

5. Fold corner to centre. Repeat behind.

6. Fold corner to centre. Repeat behind.

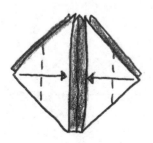

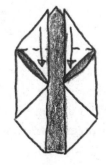

7. Fold then unfold.
Repeat behind.

8. Using the creases
made in step 7, tuck the
small triangles in the
pockets (between the
layers) of the larger
triangles. Repeat behind.

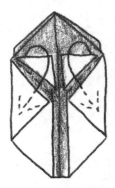

9. To inflate the waterbomb,
blow into
the hole
at the
bottom.

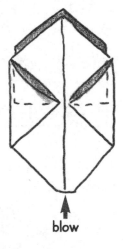

blow

When it is finished your
waterbomb should look like
this. Fill it up, and give your
friend a good soaking!

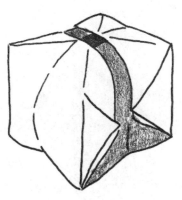

HOW TO TELL IF A PERSON IS LYING

As the person is telling you his or her version of events, keep your ears and eyes open for tell-tale signs.

1. Unusual stuttering or stammering could be an indication that the person is lying and may suggest that they are nervous.

2. Note any changes in the person's pattern of speech. See if they seem high-pitched, put on a silly voice, speak particularly quickly or slowly, or use unusual words. For instance, does it sound as though the person has learnt their story off by heart?

3. Watch out for visible signs of stress or nervousness – sweating, twitching, scratching, rubbing, looking away, shifting around, crossing and uncrossing the legs, rapid breathing – all of these indicate that the person might not be telling the whole truth.

4. There are other signs to consider. Get the person to go over the story again – but not in sequence. Ask searching questions. Does he or she seem confused? Or apparently contradicting him or herself? Ask about unimportant details (along the lines of 'What colour was his T-shirt?'). Someone who is telling the truth is less likely to get muddled and anxious, even though they might have forgotten some of the details.

5. Some say that if the 'suspect', when questioned, looks to the left, they are inventing and if they look to the right they are remembering. Perhaps you could put this theory to the test.

HOW TO TURN CARTWHEELS

To perform a well-executed cartwheel you have to be quick and approach the turn with energy and confidence.

1. Stand with your right leg in front, knees bent slightly and arms up straight.

2. Reach forward and down with your right arm, throwing your left leg up as you do so.

3. Your left arm will follow very quickly, and as, or just before, it touches the ground, kick your right leg up in the air also. For a brief moment you are in a handstand.

4. Land with your right leg first, push with your hands, bring the other foot down and stand up straight. Try to keep a rhythm ('hand, hand, foot, foot').

If you find yourself flopping to one side before you have completed the cartwheel, you could try practising beside a wall, this will discourage your legs from going down in front of or behind you.

HOW TO WRITE A LETTER

1. Start with your address at the top right of the page. Below it, to the left, put the name and address of the person you are writing to. Put the day's date on the line below that and on the right-hand side of the page.

2. Below and to the left, address the person you are writing to. If you know the person well, start with 'Dear/Dearest Daddy' (or similar). If the letter is more formal, start with 'Dear Mr/Mrs Smith', or 'Dear Sirs/Dear Sir or Madam'.

3. Leave a line and on the next line, starting at the left, begin writing your letter. Remember to use paragraphs and always check your spelling – get into the habit of using a dictionary. Whether you are typing or writing by hand, make sure the page is nicely spaced.

4. End your letter on a new line to the left of the centre. If it is to a parent or friend close your letter with: 'Love from', 'With love', or even 'Hugs and kisses'. If it is to someone you don't know quite as well leave it at: 'With affectionate greetings' or 'With best wishes'. 'With best wishes' can also be used to finish more formal letters, often followed by sign-offs, such as:
– to someone whose name you know: 'Yours sincerely';
– to someone whose name you do not know (i.e. Sir or Madam): 'Yours faithfully'.

5. When addressing the envelope, make sure it is clear and readable, and use a different line for each separate part of the address.

HOW TO BUNNY HOP

Being able to hop with your bike and lift both wheels off the ground is a great skill.

Start by hopping the bike over a line on the ground, then move on to using a thin stick, and then steadily increase your hopping height. Don't forget to wear kneepads, elbowpads, gloves and a fitted helmet for safety.

1. Stand on the bike's pedals and start pedalling until you get to about 8kph (5mph).

2. Lean the upper part of your body over the handlebars, keeping your weight centred.

3. Get your pedals level, so that your feet are parallel to the ground.

4. As you prepare for your hop, press down on the handlebars and pedals. Push your feet down, back, and then up, in one motion.

5. As you move your feet upwards, lessen the pressure of your feet and hands slightly but maintain contact between yourself and the bike. Crouch down on the bike and hop into the air.

6. Land as lightly as you can, taking the impact in your arms and legs, not your back.

HOW TO SHAKE OFF A TAIL

'A tail' is slang for a person secretly following someone else to observe their movements. Your first task is to find out if you are being followed, and if so, by whom. Your second task is to lose them.

Most amateur tails will follow behind you, trying not to be spotted.

1. If you think you are being followed, occasionally stop as you walk around – perhaps to tie a shoelace, look for something in a pocket, admire something in a shop window, and so on. Casually scan people behind you – possibly on the other side of the road – and make a rough note of anyone within distance, especially such things as height, colour of clothes, type of coat etc.; look too for anyone you recognize from earlier on in your day. Stop again after a few hundred yards and take a casual glance round, as before – is anyone still there?

2. If there is, continue walking, but this time try going somewhere that most people would not go – use your ingenuity. Stop and look in shop windows, or pause to admire a shiny car or van (choose dark-coloured ones) – you can use the reflection on these surfaces to see who's behind you. Or pull out a comb and peer into the wing mirror of a parked car or motorbike, as though about to tidy up your hair – is there anyone whose reflection you recognize? If you're still not sure, try dawdling along and then suddenly stop dead (as though you'd suddenly forgotten something vitally important) and

let everyone else walk past you – is there anyone who has also stopped and who seems to be waiting?

3. Once you are certain you are being followed, make a note of what the person looks like. At the same time, make a plan for losing him or her.

4. When you are out of sight, change your own distinguishing features: if you're wearing a coat, take it off; if you're carrying a bag, hide it in your shirt; if you're wearing a hat, stuff it in your pocket, or if you've got a hat in a pocket, put it on.

5. Speed up: do this not by quickening your pace, but by lengthening your strides – if your pace is $30^1/_2$cm (1ft) long, and you lengthen it to 41cm (16ins), in 91m (100yds) you'll have travelled an extra $30^1/_2$m ($33^1/_3$yds).

6. Dodge about: enter a large shop and immediately leave by another exit; go down a narrow alley and, while out of sight of your tail, sprint round a corner and double back on your tracks, resuming your normal pace once you're back on a main street. Jump on a bus just as it's about to shut its doors – the possibilities are endless.

7. As a last resort, hide: dodge about until you're out of your tail's sight; the moment you are, duck into a deep doorway, crouch down behind a parked car or a low wall, duck into the hallway of a large building – in short, anywhere that he or she will hurry past hoping to catch up with you again. Remember, your tail will be anxious not to lose you, and in that state of mind will probably overlook something right under his or her nose.

HOW TO LASSO LIKE A COWBOY

To make your lasso you will need about 10m (33ft) of stiff cord (the rope), a large needle and some thin string.

Take one end of the rope and make a small loop. It needs to be big enough for the rope to pass through it easily – but not much bigger than that. Instead of tying, sew the end to the rope with the string to make a permanent loop at one end. This loop is called a 'honda'.

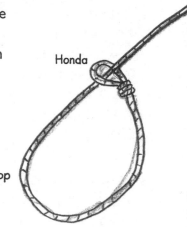

Honda

Loop

Preparing and throwing the lasso:

1. Take position in front of your target, a post or tree stump for instance. Pull the loose end of the rope through the honda. Stop when you have about 3m (10ft) left to feed through. This will be the loop you use to snare your target.

2. Coil the loose end of the rope and hold it in one hand. Leave about 1¹/₂m (5ft) between the coil and the loop to allow you to swing your lasso.

3. Hold the loop-end of the rope in your free hand, about 20cm (8ins) from where the loop runs through the honda.

4. Spin the lasso over your head with clockwise turns of your hand, tracing a circle in the air. Let your wrist act as an axle, and swing the rope as if it were a wheel spinning horizontally around your wrist and over your head.

5. When you feel ready to rope your target, give a quick step forward, bring your hand forward and down to the level of your shoulder, let it stretch to a full arm's length without interrupting the swinging motion of the loop, and let it go at your target. The loop should sail straight at your target without losing its circular form.

6. Now to snare the wild, kicking buffalo, or escaping cowboy criminal.

HOW TO MAKE A VOLCANO

This is a messy project and needs space, so if you can, make it outdoors or cover your work area with newspaper.

You will need: modelling clay (brown and red are best), baking soda, red food colouring, washing-up liquid, vinegar.

1. Make a volcano shape with the modelling clay. Use brown clay for the base and red clay for the rim to look like hot lava. If you can't find red clay, colour a small amount with the food colouring.

2. Scoop out a hole in the top of the volcano for the crater. Put 1 tablespoon of baking soda, a few drops of red food colouring and a few drops of washing-up liquid in the crater.

3. Pour in $^1/_4$ cup of vinegar, stand well back and watch the volcano erupt.

HOW TO FIND ORION

The constellation Orion, the Hunter, can be seen all over the world because it lies on the celestial equator. Even if you haven't identified them in the night sky, you may have heard of some of the stars that make up this constellation, including Rigel and Betelgeuse.

1. Look towards the south if you are in the northern hemisphere, north if you are in the southern hemisphere.

2. Find Orion's belt – three stars in a short, straight line.

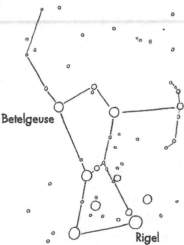

3. Look for Orion's knee to the lower right – it's the bright star, Rigel.

4. Locate the orange-red star, Betelgeuse, at the upper left from the belt, often called 'Beetlejuice'.

HOW TO BOWL A SPINNER

Spin bowling is one of the most skilful bowling techniques in the game of cricket. The spin bowler uses the wrist and fingers to make the ball spin as it leaves the hand. The spin causes the ball to change direction once it lands.
This makes it harder for the batsman to hit the ball, and can sometimes turn the ball from its path onto the wicket. In addition, a spinning ball may often come off the bat at an unpredictable angle, leading to the batsman being caught out.

There are two main types of spin bowling – off-spin and leg-spin.

A few general tips. Play with a cricket ball as often as you can – throw it up and down, twisting your wrist to make the ball spin in the air. Bear in mind that you can probably get more spin with a worn ball, so when playing a match try not to use a brand-new ball. When bowling, keep your arms close to your body. Bring your bowling arm down quickly and release the ball as high as you can, so the flight of the ball causes the batsman to lift his head up and then down, which may put him off his stroke.

Off-spin. Twist your hand in a clockwise direction as you let go of the ball so that when it hits the pitch it spins to your right. The spin is generated by the three middle fingers, with the middle joints of your fingers resting on the seam of the ball. As you bowl, turn your wrist clockwise to generate the spin on the ball. Use your first two fingers to deliver the ball.

Leg-spin. Twist the ball anti-clockwise and release it from the palm so that it rolls over the base of your little finger. It will spin to your left when it lands. Hold the ball with the top joints of the index and second fingers across the seam, the ball resting between a bent third finger and the thumb. As you release the ball, straighten your fingers; much of the work on the ball will be done by the third finger, turning the ball anti-clockwise. Flick your wrist so your palm faces downwards.

HOW TO BEND IT LIKE BECKHAM

1. Approach the ball at an angle. Place your standing foot (rather than your kicking foot) close to the ball, facing the direction you want the ball to go. Start by practising this as you go to kick the ball.

2. Once you're comfortable with this, try to 'bend it'. If you kick with your right foot, to send the ball from right to left, strike the bottom half of the right-hand side with the inside, top half of your foot. To curve the ball from left to right, strike the bottom half of the left side of the ball with the outside of your foot. (Reverse these moves if you kick with your left foot.) To swerve a ball with the outside of your foot, strike 'across' the ball.

HOW TO MAKE A WATER CLOCK

You will need five paper cups of the same size, five drawing pins, a sturdy piece of cardboard, a glass jar as big as the cup, a narrow strip of paper, glue, a stopwatch, and a pencil.

1. Use a drawing pin to prick a hole in the bottom of each cup.

2. Pin the five cups to the cardboard, one under the other. Leave a three-finger gap between each cup.

3. Stick the strip of paper vertically to the glass jar and put the jar under the bottom cup.

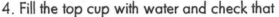

4. Fill the top cup with water and check that it drips through each cup into the jar at the bottom.

5. OK? Then do it again, using the same water, but this time start your stopwatch at the moment you start pouring.

6. At intervals of five minutes, mark the water level on the paper on your jar.

7. When all the water has dripped into the jar, you can use this 'clock' to keep track of time.

HOW TO FREEZE A FINGER

Make a bet with a friend that if you point to one of their fingers and ask them to wiggle it, that finger will freeze and they will wiggle the wrong one instead. If they accept the bet, tell them to put their arms out and cross them at the wrists. They should then turn their palms together and interlock their fingers. Now ask them to bring their hands in towards their stomach, and continue moving their hands round and upwards until their interlocked fingers are on top. Now point to one of their fingers (don't actually touch it) and see if they know which one to wiggle. Most likely, they will be confused and wiggle the wrong one. The third and fourth finger on each hand is the hardest to figure out, so start with those if you want to win the bet.

HOW TO GAG A KNOW-ALL

'Did you know that your brain's 80 per cent water?'

(This is fact, not an insult.)

HOW TO BE A MATHS MAGICIAN

1. Ask a friend to think of a three-digit number. The only condition is that the first digit and the last digit must differ by more than one – for example 364 would not do because there is a difference of only one between the first and last digits (3 and 4).

2. Your friend might need a calculator – you, of course, do not. Now tell your friend to reverse the number. Let's say he or she chose 469 – reversing it would give 964.

3. Now tell your friend to subtract the smaller number from the larger (964 − 469 = 495). All this is done without your knowing what any of the numbers are.

4. Tell your friend now to take the result of this subtraction (495 in our example) and reverse it (594), and then to add the result and its reverse together.

5. Your turn now. You announce the answer: 1089.

You will be right every time!

HOW TO WARM YOUR FEET UP

Sprinkle a pinch of ground cayenne pepper into your socks. It will warm your feet without burning them. But be sure that any cuts, blisters and scratches on your feet are covered with a sticking plaster, and be very careful not to allow the pepper to touch your eyes, or the nose and mouth area, as it might sting or at least feel uncomfortably hot.

HOW TO CLIMB A ROPE

To most people, a long rope with no knots
to grip looks impossible to climb. Here's
how to escape the gym teacher and
wriggle up the rope like a boa constrictor:

1. Stand in front of the rope and reach
up with both arms – they should be well
above your head, but slightly bent at the
elbows to give you the necessary leverage.

2. Grasp the rope and pull yourself up.
As you do so, cross your legs round
the rope and grip it between your thighs
and again between your feet.

3. Reach up again, one arm at a time.
Pull yourself up with your hands while using
the grip between your feet and thighs
to push up.

HOW TO MAKE A BOOMERANG

Boomerangs do not have to be single angled pieces of
wood. They were traditionally that shape because they
were made from bent pieces of wood. If you make one out
of cardboard, an X-shape boomerang is far more effective.

You will need: cardboard, a ruler, scissors, glue or stapler,
coloured markers (to decorate).

1. Measure and cut two lengths of cardboard 20 x 3cm
(8 x 1¼ins). Make sure the sides of each length are

parallel and that the two lengths are identical to each other. Cut the eight corners so that they are nicely rounded.

2. Fold up the end of each wing about 2cm ($^3/_4$in) from the tip, to make a rough right angle.

3. Lay one piece across the other to form an X, crossing them in the centre and at right angles. Glue or staple them together at the centre. Decorate your creation.

4. To throw, hold your boomerang vertically by one of its blades so the folded tips bend toward you. Raise your arm and throw it with a quick snap of your wrist using just a little force.

5. If it doesn't work after several tries, adjust the folded ends. You could also try placing four pea-sized blobs of tacky putty on the underside of each wing about three-quarters of the length from the centre. Soon it'll whizz back to you every time.

HOW TO DOWSE FOR WATER

Dowsing is a way of locating something that is hidden. A person – the dowser – using a rod, stick or other device known as a dowsing rod or 'wishing rod', can determine the exact location of such things as underground water, buried treasure, oil, lost objects and even people. Since the art of dowsing has never been scientifically proven, it is considered as a type of divination.

Traditional dowsing rods were made from forked hazel branches, although the wood of apple, beech and alder are said to work as well. Alternatively, L-shaped copper or iron rods are used – or, unmystical as it sounds, wire coat hangers.

To make dowsing rods out of wire hangers, you need the long horizontal wire (the bit over which you might drape a pair of trousers) and about 10cm (4ins) of one angled side. Take two hangers and cut from them this angled length using a pair of wire cutters. Bend each of the short sides out a little to form a right-angle or L-shape. The shorter end is the handle: over each handle fit half a plastic drinking straw to form a sleeve (this allows the rod to swivel freely without being affected by your hand).

To dowse with your L-shaped rods, hold a rod in each hand, horizontally in front of you. When you're over water the rods will cross each other, apparently moving of their own accord, pointing towards the spot where the water can be found.

HOW TO JUMPSHOOT A BASKETBALL

1. Start with both feet flat on the floor. With your body facing the basket, crouch down low – this will give you the momentum to jump.

2. Rise up off your feet. Make sure you can see the rim of the hoop. Your shooting hand should cup the ball and point towards the basket, while your other hand can gently guide the shot, loosely holding the side of the ball.

3. Keep your elbows in and your eyes on a spot over the front of the rim. Bend the wrist of your shooting hand backwards, the ball resting on the pads of your fingers.

4. As you spring off the ground, extend your arms, raising the ball smoothly in one fluid motion.

5. At the top of the jump, snap your wrist forward and let go of the ball.

6. At the end of the shot, when the ball flies through the hoop, your fingers should be pointing down to the floor.

HOW TO MAKE FIRE

1. Rapidly twirling a dry twig round inside a hole in a plank of wood or a dead tree trunk will produce enough heat to set light to dry moss.

2. Cutting a slot into a piece of bamboo and wearing down this slot with another piece of bamboo will work off fragments of the wood. The friction will set these shavings on fire.

3. Striking a stone against a flint will create sparks which, if they fall onto dry moss, can set it alight.

4. If it is bright and sunny you can set paper, dry moss or grass alight by holding a magnifying glass over it and drawing it upwards until the circle of sunlight the glass makes on the area is a tiny bright point. Hold it there and a tiny curl of smoke will soon appear, and then flames.

HOW TO RECOGNIZE A WITCH

According to the children's author Roald Dahl, witches dress and look just like normal women. Luckily there are ways to spot a witch:

They wear gloves because they have claws that need hiding. They are bald and wear wigs. They have larger nostrils than ordinary people. The pupil in the middle of their eyes changes colour from fire to ice. They don't have toes, so they have to wear wide shoes with square ends. They have blue spit.

HOW TO SPEED-READ

When you read, it is not necessary to look at every letter of a word to know what the word is; you don't even have to see the word in detail, as you know by its shape and length and by its context (the meaning of the rest of the sentence in which it appears) what it is. To speed-read you have to be able to scan the lines you are reading. The brain soon learns which words are the important ones and also learns to take in several words together.

To speed up your reading, run your finger along beneath each line you read. Gradually increase the speed of your finger and you'll find your reading speeds up too. Don't hurry this, though, or you just won't take in what you're reading.

To progress your speed-reading, use a newspaper, as columns are narrower than book pages. Draw a line right down the centre of a column. Now try to read each line of words without moving your eyes from the beginning to the end of the line but by looking at its centre. You'll find that, with practice, your eyes are taking in a complete line at a time – and if you continue, you'll find that your brain starts doing the same and you can fully understand what you're reading. After a while don't draw the line and you'll soon be able to read a newspaper column just by running your eyes down the centre.

Avoid saying the words to yourself, and going back over something you've just read. Doing so will slow you down.

HOW TO SURVIVE AN EARTHQUAKE

Fortunately the great majority of the earthquakes that are occurring around us nearly all the time are so slight that only seismographs register them. Stronger earthquakes, however, can cause a great deal of damage.

1. If you are indoors and have time, turn off all gas- and fire-related equipment (a gas fire or cooker, for instance). Stay indoors. Drop down to the floor and take cover under a strong table or desk. Hold on to it and, if necessary, move with it. Failing suitable pieces of furniture, stand in a doorway. Keep clear of windows, glass, fireplaces, and heavy furniture or appliances. Stay put until the shaking stops and it's safe to move.

2. If you're outside, if possible get out into the open. Stay away from buildings, trees, power lines, bridges, high walls and rocks.

3. If you're in a car, urge everyone to stay in the vehicle. Ask the driver to keep the car away from traffic, bridges, overpasses and tunnels, trees, lamp posts, power lines and road signs, and to stop the car where it seems safe.

4. After the shaking has stopped, check for any injured people and make sure they're as comfortable and safe as possible; check for hazards – fire, water leakages, damaged structures – turn off power supplies if a gas leak is suspected or electrical wiring is damaged, and clean up dangerous spills. Only use the telephone for emergencies and keep listening to the radio. Expect aftershocks and even tidal waves (seismic sea waves).

The Richter Scale measures an earthquake's strength:

1–3	Generally not felt but recorded on seismographs
3–4	Felt, but damage very rare
4–5	Widely felt, some local damage, not significant
5–6	Damage to poorly constructed buildings
6–7	Destructive – a fair amount of damage
7–8	Major – serious damage over large areas
8–9	Great – widespread destruction and loss of life
9–plus	Rare – causes great destruction over huge area

HOW TO LOCATE A THUNDERSTORM

Water droplets colliding inside storm clouds cause electrons to move so quickly that a large electrical spark is created. This is lightning. The air along its path is heated so intensely and expands so much that it creates a very loud noise – thunder. But although lightning and thunder occur together, we see the lightning some time before we hear the thunder because the speed of light is about a million times that of sound.

It is possible to estimate how far away a thunderstorm is by counting the number of seconds between the lightning flash and the thunderclap. Divide what you get by three and that will give you the approximate distance in kilometres.

HOW TO MAKE A PAPER PLANE

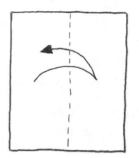

1. Take an A4 sheet of paper and crease it along the middle, by folding it in half lengthwise.

2. Fold down the top corners inward to the centre crease, making two right-angle triangles. Fold the large top triangle over and down.

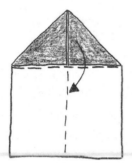

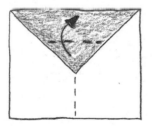

3. Fold the lower part of the tip of the large triangle up again. But not quite up to the top.

4. Fold the top corners inward to the centre crease and then unfold them.

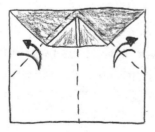

5. Now bisect the new folds you made, using the previous creases as a guide. Fold and unfold along the two dashed lines.

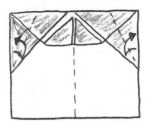

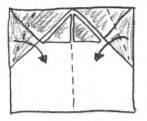

6. Now fold the two large right-angle triangles down again.

7. Fold inwards along the two dotted and dashed folds, tucking the triangles well underneath, snugly locking them in place.

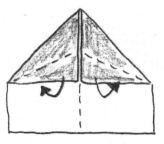

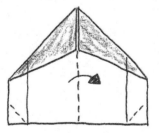

8. Now make a few extra folds. Where you see the dotted and dashed lines in the diagram, fold these wings inwards. Fold the small triangles outwards to make winglets that help balance the plane in flight.

Top tip. This is a slow and graceful flyer. It flies best if you don't throw it hard, but simply release it as your hand moves forward a little.

HOW TO ROW A BOAT

It is a good idea not to go off alone in a boat – take a friend with you. Make sure you are prepared – that you are both wearing life jackets and that the boat is dry and in good condition.

1. Sit with your back to the bow (the front of the boat) and your feet against the foot board, your legs slightly bent at the knee. Place an oar in each rowlock – the U-shaped metal fittings that fit into holes in the boat's side to hold the oars.

2. If you have a companion, he or she should get into the boat and sit at the back – that is, on the stern thwart. Get him or her to push the boat off from the bank or jetty so that it drifts out.

3. With your arms straight out in front of you, hold the oar handles with your wrists dropped so that the oar blades are parallel to and just above the surface of the water. Keep your back straight and look directly in front of you, which, when you're rowing, is over the stern (the back of the boat).

4. Lower the blades into the water and, at the same time, straighten your wrists – this will set the blades at right angles to the surface as they enter.

5. Lean back and bring the oar handles towards your chest, completing the stroke by bending your arms. Your weight, and the effort of your legs, more than the strength of your arms, pull the blades through the water, making the

boat move in the opposite direction. So you are effectively going backwards.

6. As the stroke ends, lift the blades from the water, straighten your arms and lean forwards again – this will bring the blades back to the starting point again.

7. Lower the blades into the water and take another stroke, and so on. The hardest strokes are the first six or seven; once the boat is actually under way, less effort is needed to keep it travelling at the same pace.

8. Pulling harder on one oar will make the boat turn away from that side – i.e. if you pull on your right oar, the boat will move towards your left (which is to the boat's right, since you're facing backwards).

9. To slow or stop the boat, drop the blades into the water and brace yourself against them – the flat blades will act as brakes. To move the boat backwards, hold that position and then push against the oar handles, so that the blades move through the water in the opposite direction. As the blades near the bow, lift them out of the water, lean back and drop them in again to take another stroke – in effect, rowing in reverse.

If for any reason the boat should be upset and you end up in the water – don't panic! Your life jacket will keep you afloat. Stay close to the boat until help arrives or until you and your friend can push it to the bank by holding on to one side and kicking with your legs. You can climb back in provided your friend is holding on to the other side as you do so, to counterbalance your weight.

HOW TO TELL WHICH WAY IS NORTH

You will need: a wristwatch with hands, set to the correct local time. You need to be able to see the sun (even if it's shining through cloud). Most important of all, you also need to know that the sun rises in the east and sets in the west; and that at 12 noon in the northern hemisphere it is due south (in the southern hemisphere it's due north).

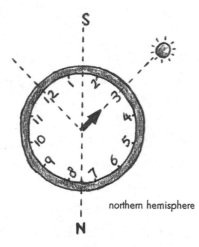

northern hemisphere

1. With the watch horizontal, aim the hour hand at the sun. Then exactly divide the angle between the position of the hour hand and the 12 on the watch face – the line that follows that angle is the north–south line. Since you know the position of the sun at noon, and you know the time, you can then work out which way is north and which south.

2. If you have a digital watch, draw a watch face on a piece of paper, mark the 12 and then draw in the hour hand in the position for the time shown on your digital. Next, aim the hour hand in the drawing at the sun and follow the procedure as for a watch with hands (technically termed an analogue watch).

3. If you are in the southern hemisphere, aim the 12 on the

watch face at the sun and find the north-south line by bisecting the angle between the hour hand and 12. Remember that in this hemisphere, the sun will be due north at noon; otherwise, exactly the same principles apply as for the northern hemisphere.

HOW TO GET AN EGG INTO A BOTTLE

You will need: a peeled, hard-boiled egg, a plastic or glass bottle with an opening slightly smaller than the egg, and a large jug of hot water.

1. To hard-boil an egg put it in a saucepan, cover with water and simmer it for eight to ten minutes. Then put it in cold water and leave it for at least another ten minutes to cool down. When the egg has cooled down, tap it gently until the shell cracks. Peel it carefully. At the end you should have a smooth, unblemished white oval.

2. Heat the bottle, inside and out, by filling it with hot water. Pour out the water and then quickly place the egg, pointed side down, in the bottle opening.

3. As the air inside the bottle cools, the egg will slowly move into the bottle.

4. To get the egg out, hold the bottle upside-down so that the egg is near the opening. Blow hard into the bottle with your mouth tight against the opening. The egg will vibrate, but then act as a seal, trapping air inside. Point the bottle away from yourself and watch the egg fly out.

108

HOW TO TIE A KNOT WITH ONE HAND

1. Drape the string over your hand.

2. Bend your hand, and with your first and second fingers, pick up the string which is hanging behind your hand.

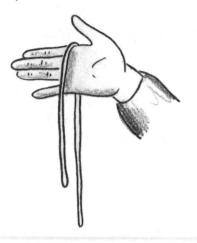

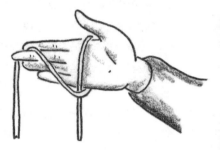

3. Flick your wrist down, so the string on top of your hand slides off the front of your fingers.

Hey presto, a knot.

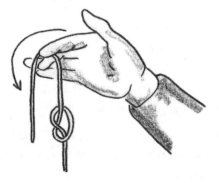

HOW TO RIDE A UNICYCLE

1. Get two friends to stand either side of you and get up on the unicycle with your arms around their shoulders. Check that the unicycle is the correct height by sitting on the saddle and placing one foot on a pedal at the lowest point. You should be able to reach that pedal with your leg very slightly bent.

2. Sit up straight and look straight ahead. Your weight should be on the seat, not on the pedals. Rock the pedals to get a sense of balance, and then bring the pedals round so that they're parallel with the ground.

3. Still holding on to your helpers, pedal a half-turn, then stop. Do this a few times before going on to pedal full turns. Doing lots of half-turns (from pedals level to pedals level again) is harder than continuous pedalling, but keeps you in control of the movement.

4. Switch from holding on to your helpers' shoulders to holding their wrists, and then to holding the wrist of just one helper.

5. Let go of both helpers and switch to using a wall instead. Pedal a half-turn forwards, sliding your hand along the wall. Build this up into a whole turn, two turns and so on until you are comfortable sliding along the wall with only a very light hold on it.

6. To turn the unicycle, swivel your body and the unicycle in the direction you want to go, but be careful to avoid leaning to the side.

HOW TO DRAW A CARTOON

If you can draw a basic face shape, it is very easy to adjust certain features to give each of your cartoons a different personality. Start with a basic oval, then add other circles for the nose and eyes. Then simply decorate with different-shaped mouths, and try moving the eyeballs or eyebrows, or adding hair or glasses. See what expressions you can create. You will soon begin to build a library of faces with different and hilarious personalities.

HOW TO MAKE YOUR OWN TRUMP CARDS

1. Cut out a playing-card-size piece of white card for each of your friends. If you have 20 friends, you will need 20 pieces of card.

2. At the top of each piece of card write the name of a friend, and either draw a picture or stick a photo of them beneath their name.

3. Write the categories shown below on each of the cards:

4. Assess your friends' performance in each of the categories, and write an appropriate number by each category on their card. For example, if one of your friends is good enough to play in the next World Cup, he'll score a ten out of ten beside 'Footballing skills'.

Days per year spent wearing shorts:	43
Ability to get out of trouble:	8
Smelliness of farts:	10
Footballing skills.	5
Maximum days without washing.	4
Den-building skills.	7
Number of magic tricks known.	1
Ability to whistle.	10

5. Shuffle the cards and deal them out between players.

6. Starting with the top card in your pile, choose a category and read out its score.

7. Moving round the circle in a clockwise direction, each player then reads out their score for that category. The person with the highest score wins all the cards from that round and places them at the bottom of his pile. He then chooses the category for the next round.

8. One by one, players will lose all of their cards. The winner is the player who ends up with the whole pack.

HOW TO WRITE A LIMERICK

A limerick is a poem with five lines. It always has the same rhyming pattern and rhythm. The first, second and fifth lines usually have eight syllables each, and the final syllables of each of these lines rhyme. The middle lines both have five or six syllables and a different rhyme.

1. Begin by picking a boy or girl's name and write an eight-syllable line with that name at the end. For example: 'There once was a young man called Matt,'

2. Make a list of words that rhyme with the last syllable in the first line – for instance, hat, cat, fat, sat, pat, rat. Now write a second eight-syllable line ending with one of your rhyming words. For example: 'Whose pet was a rat in a hat.'

3. Now think of a story for your character and write two five-syllable lines with words that rhyme at the end. For example: 'The rat said, 'You know, /The hat has to go,'

4. For the final line, which will be eight syllables long, think of a resolution for your story. Go back to your list of rhyming words and be as silly as you want. 'A cat wears a hat, not a rat.'

HOW TO MILK A COW

1. Clean your hands.

2. Put a dollop of udder cream on your hands.

3. Take the base of the cow's teat firmly between the last three fingers of your left hand.

4. Draw slightly on the teat and the udder at the same time.

5. Do not jerk or pull – this will irritate the cow and can cause injury.

6. With your right hand, take the base of another teat firmly between the last three fingers and repeat as above.

7. Proceed quickly but gently with each hand until the supply of milk finishes.

Top tip. Never milk a cow when it is eating.

HOW TO DRIBBLE A BASKETBALL

You are not allowed to run with the ball so dribbling is a crucial skill. You may only use one hand at a time and once you have stopped dribbling you must pass or shoot.

1. Gain control of the ball by spreading your fingers over its top.

2. Begin the dribble by pushing the ball firmly to the floor. Use your hand and wrist to control the height and speed of the bounce.

3 Keep your hand on top of the ball so that it rebounds accurately, and keep the bounce height to waist level. Try not to let the ball hit the palm of your hand. Feel the ball with your fingers and let your wrists do the work.

4. Move forward on the balls of your feet and bend your knees to maintain your balance.

Top tip. Keep your body over the ball to shield the ball from your opponents. To help keep possession, dribble with the hand farthest away from your opponent.

HOW TO KEEP PEOPLE IN SUSPENSE

A 'cliffhanger' is anything in a story, article, radio or TV programme, or film that leaves a listener, reader or viewer in suspense – the hero is left hanging from a cliff, in deadly danger of his life. It is a trick used to keep people's attention – by being kept in suspense, they want to know more.

You can use similar tricks to become the best teller (or writer) of jokes, stories, and even speeches, and hold your audience in suspense:

1. Don't give too much away too early. Quickly ending an account with something like 'Suddenly shots rang out and they all fell dead. The End' leaves people disappointed and frustrated.

2. Never rush. Spin the tale out (but don't go so slowly that it becomes boring). Pause occasionally – this often makes people say 'Go on!' or 'What happened next?'

3. Change direction. Just as you get to a good bit, say something like, 'Meanwhile, as the phantom bus bore down on us, Gran was making Eccles cakes at home ...'

4. Break off your story occasionally. 'Then suddenly a huge black shape appeared in front of him and he – oh, there goes the bell. Tell you later.'

5. Leave the best part to the end, but build the drama up bit by bit.

HOW TO MAKE A FORTUNE FINDER

To make a fortune finder all you need is a square piece of paper and some coloured pens.

1. Fold the square in half from one corner to the other.

2. Fold it again, to form a smaller triangle. Then unfold the sheet and lay it flat.

3. Fold each corner of the square into the middle, so the corners all meet at the centre.

4. Turn the fortune finder over, and repeat step 3, folding the new corners into the middle.

5. Turn the sheet over so that you can see four squares, and fold in half with the squares on the outside.

6. Finally, keeping the squares on the outside, fold in half the other way.

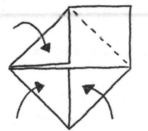

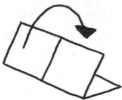

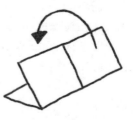

7. Use coloured pens to put a different-coloured blob on each of the four outer squares.

8. Write a different number on each of the eight inner triangles.

9. Lift up each of the numbered triangles and write a fortune, such as 'You will be rich and famous' or 'You will live in another country' underneath.

10. Slide the thumb and forefinger of both your hands under the flaps of your fortune finder.

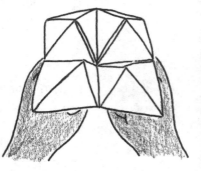

11. Ask a friend to choose one of the colours on the flaps of your fortune finder. Spell out the colour, opening and closing the fortune finder for each letter.

On the last letter, hold the fortune finder open and ask your friend to choose one of the four numbers that show inside.

12. Count out that number, opening and closing the fortune finder, then ask your friend to choose another number and count it out the same way.

13. Ask your friend to pick a final number. Open up the flap beneath that number and read your friend's fortune.

You can use fortune finders for lots of other things by changing what you write under the number flaps. Instead of writing fortunes you could try dares, questions, insults, the names of your friends or anything else you can think of.

HOW TO KEEP A SECRET DIARY

1. Make sure that your diary is special to you. You might want to cover a blank pad with paper, fabric or photos.

2. Don't feel that you have to write something every day.

3. Focus on the details of your day: who you saw, what you did, where you went and how you felt.

4. Don't whinge in it. Write boldly.

5. If you are writing sensational material about people you know, disguise their identities with code names.

6. It may help to address your entries to an imaginary person.

7. Keep it somewhere safe and away from prying eyes.

8. Just to be extra sure that no one will ever read it, write something like MY BOOK OF ALGEBRA on the cover.

HOW TO PROVE YOU'RE NOT BIG-HEADED

So people say you've got a big head and that you think you are the best at everything? How do you prove them wrong? Simple – you put your head through a playing card.

1. Fold an old playing card down the middle lengthways and crease it hard along the fold.

2. With a pair of scissors, make eight evenly spaced cuts along the folded edge, but make sure you stop before you reach the far edge.

3. Turn the card around and make seven cuts along the open edge, in between the first set of cuts. Don't cut through the folded edge.

4. Flatten out the card and cut carefully along the crease from A to B. Now open out the card gently into a large, ragged ring, and put your head through it.

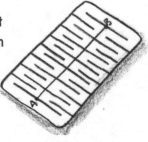

HOW TO SEND A MESSAGE BY SEMAPHORE

Semaphore is a code that uses different arm positions to represent each of the letters in the alphabet. To start a message, cross your arms in front of you with your elbows straight and hands pointing to the ground. This position means 'Attention' or 'End of Message'. Spell out your message letter by letter using the positions below below. The black flag shows the position of your left arm, and the white your right arm.

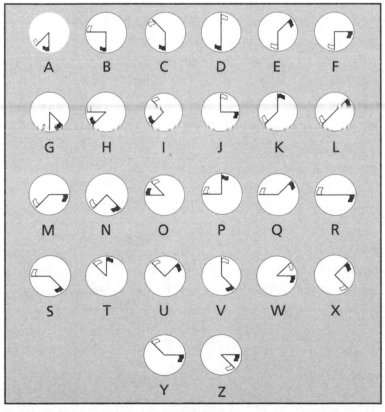

HOW TO WIN AT CONKERS

Conkers is a two-player game. Each player is armed with a conker hanging from a piece of string. The aim is to annihilate your opponent's conker before they destroy yours.

1. To prepare your conker, drill a hole through the centre from top to bottom. Then thread a piece of string 30cm (1ft) long through the hole. Tie a couple of knots below the conker to keep it in place.

2. Challenge a fellow conker-owner to a match and flip a coin to decide who will go first.

3. If your opponent is going first, wrap the end of your string tightly around your hand and let the conker dangle down. Your opponent may then choose the height at which you hold the conker, and must try to hit it with his own. If he misses, he has two more attempts before it is your turn.

4. When it's your turn, keep the end of the string wrapped around your hand as before, then take the conker in your other hand and draw it back, ready to strike. Release the conker and swing it down as hard and fast as you can against your opponent's conker. Don't hurt yourself.

5. Continue taking it in turns to hit each other's conker until one of them is destroyed.

ADDITIONAL RULES

1. If the strings become tangled, the first player to shout 'Strings!' gets an extra go.

2. If when you hit your opponent's conker it swings in a complete circle, you get an extra go.

3. If you drop your conker immediately shout 'No stamps!' If you do not manage to do this before your opponent shouts 'Stamps!' your opponent may stamp on your conker.

TIPS FOR WINNING

1. Choose a big, symmetrical conker.

2. Avoid conkers with cracks or white spots on them.

3. Check that your conker sinks straight to the bottom of a glass of water, and discard any that float.

4. Bake your conker in an oven.

5. Soak your conker in vinegar.

6. Coat your conker with a layer of matt varnish.

7. Use a conker from a previous year.

HOW TO FIND FOSSILS AND TREASURE

Wherever you are, you may be standing on a fossil: perhaps bones, teeth, eggs, frozen mammoth flesh or fossilized fur. And there are other kinds of fascinating treasure to discover too, such as Bronze Age artefacts, Roman coins, jewellery and pottery.

You don't have to be an archaeologist or palaeontologist

to uncover the remains of ancient life – you just need to be observant, patient and lucky.

Where to look:

1. **Beaches**. Look in the shingle and under rocks as well as in the sand; if there are flints check them, too – they could contain fossils.

2. **Riverbanks**. Check under stones and along the water's edge. Shallow streambeds are also worth investigating.

3. **Cliffs**. Erosion might uncover some super fossils (or Stone Age carvings), which you could find either in the cliff face or tumbled down to the foot of the cliff.

4. **Quarries**. These are good places to look, where stone and earth has been dug up to use for building (but do observe safety precautions).

5. **Farmland**. It's worth looking in farmland, too, especially fields where ploughing will have turned up the earth and all kinds of treasures that have been buried for years, or even centuries, may have come to the surface.

You will need tools to help unearth your fossils and treasure. Use a brush to remove gently any sand or soil, a small trowel to dig around your discovery, and a hammer and chisel if you are in a rocky area. Take kitchen paper with you to wrap your fossils, a camera to record your discoveries, and plastic bags so you can carry them to the museum!

HOW TO TEST YOUR TELEPATHIC POWERS

Prepare six flash cards. Each one should show a very simple picture. Here are some suggestions of what you could draw: a square, a triangle, a star, a circle, a wavy line and a spiral.

Sit back-to-back with a friend and decide who will be the sender and who will be the receiver.

The sender shuffles the flash cards. Then one by one the sender takes the top card in the pile, shouts 'Go' and concentrates really hard on 'sending' the image to the receiver.

The receiver has a pencil and paper and draws whatever comes into his mind. When all the cards have been 'sent', compare the flash cards sent by the sender to the pictures drawn by the receiver in each instance. Look for similarities. For example, a triangle may be telepathically received as the sail of a boat.

HOW TO SHAVE

1. Thoroughly wash your face.

2. Hold a hot, wet flannel against your beard for a few minutes to soften your skin.

3. Fill the sink with warm water.

4. Squirt a dollop of shaving foam onto your hands and cover your beard evenly. The longer and thicker your beard, the more shaving foam you will need.

5. Pulling your skin tight before each stroke, start at the bottom of your sideburns and pull the razor with firm, light movements towards your jaw. When shaving you should always follow the direction of the hair.

6. Frequently rinse your razor to prevent it getting clogged with hair.

7. Tuck your top lip under your teeth to stretch the skin between your mouth and your nose, then shave this area using short, downward strokes.

8. Shave your chin, then tip your head back and pull the razor from the bottom of the hairs near your throat to the tip of your chin.

9. Wash off any leftover shaving cream and check that you haven't missed any hairs.

10. Apply some cold water or aftershave, and admire yourself in the mirror.

HOW TO BE THE BEST ALL AROUND THE WORLD

If you know many languages, you can be the best around the world ... or at least people will think you are!

English	I am the best
French	Je suis le meilleur
Russian	Ya velikiy
Spanish	Soy lo mejor
Italian	Sono il migliore
Urdu	Māi sab se achā
Portuguese	Sou o melhor
German	Ich bin das Beste
Swedish	Jag är bäst
Danish	Jeg er den bedst
Greek	E-me o kaliteros
Polish	Jestem wspaniały
Arabic	Ana Al'aadham
Mandarin	Wǒ shi zuì hǎo de
Hindi	Māi sab se achā
Swahili	Mimi mbinga ni
Latin	Optimus sum

NOTE TO READERS

The publisher and authors disclaim any liability
for accidents or injuries that may occur as a
result of information given in this book.

To be the best at everything you'll need to use your
best common sense at all times: always wear
appropriate safety gear, stay within the law and
local rules, and be considerate of other people.